Customer
Relationship
Management

Customer Relationship Management (CRM)

Building the Business Case

Lynette Ryals, Simon Knox and Stan Maklan

School of Management

PEARSON EDUCATION LIMITED

Head Office:
Edinburgh Gate
Harlow CM20 2JE
Tel: +44 (0)1279 623623
Fax: +44 (0)1279 431059

London Office:
128 Long Acre
London WC2E 9AN
Tel: +44 (0)20 7447 2000
Fax: +44 (0)20 7240 5771
Website: www.business-minds.com

First published in Great Britain 2000

© Cranfield University, Institute for Advanced Research in Marketing,
Cranfield School of Management

The right of Lynette Ryals, Simon Knox and Stan Maklan to be identified
as authors of this work has been asserted by them in accordance with the
Copyright, Designs, and Patents Act 1988.

ISBN 0 273 65069 6

British Library Cataloguing in Publication Data
A CIP catalogue record for this book can be obtained from the British Library.

10 9 8 7 6 5 4 3 2 1

Typeset by Boyd Elliott Typesetting
Printed and bound in Great Britain

The Publishers' policy is to use paper manufactured from sustainable forests.

About the authors

Lynette Ryals MA (Oxon), MBA, FIIMR is a Lecturer in Marketing at the Cranfield School of Management in the UK. She joined Cranfield from a major management consultancy and specialises in marketing measurement and IT in marketing, particularly in service businesses, and is currently working towards a PhD in customer profitability.

Lynette began her career in the City as a fund manager and stockbroker trading UK equities, options and futures, and still lectures occasionally on finance issues. She then moved to a marketing company to work on corporate development and acquisitions, subsequently transferring into the consultancy arm of the same business group. She is a Registered Representative of the London Stock Exchange and is the only woman in the UK to have passed the Fellowship examinations of the Institute of Investment Analysis and Research (IIMR).

Her teaching assignments include the Cranfield MSc and MBA programmes as well as tailored corporate programmes and open programmes run at Cranfield. She was a guest lecturer for the Institute of Management in Nicosia, Cyprus, in 1993 and for the Chartered Institute of Management Accountants in Sri Lanka in 1995.

From 1 January 2000, Lynette has been the Director of the Executive MBA programme.

Email: lynette.ryals@cranfield.ac.uk

Simon Knox, BSc, PhD is Professor of Brand Marketing at the Cranfield School of Management in the UK and is a consultant to a number of multinational companies including McDonald's, Levi Strauss, DiverseyLever and the Ocean Group. Upon graduating, he followed a career in the marketing of international brands with Unilever Plc in a number of senior marketing roles in both detergents and foods.

Since joining Cranfield, Simon has published over 60 papers on branding and customer purchasing styles and is a regular speaker at international conferences. He is the Director of the Institute for Advanced Research in Marketing in the School and is currently leading a research team on Customer Relationship Management on behalf of Computer Sciences Corporation (CSC). He is the co-author of the book, *Competing on Value* (http://www.competingonvalue.com) published by Financial Times Pitman Publishing in the UK and Germany.

Email: s.knox@cranfield.ac.uk

Stan Maklan, BSc, MBA is a Managing Consultant with Computer Sciences Corporation (CSC) working in its European Customer Relationship Management (CRM) practice and its global management research centre, Research Services. Before joining its European division, he established CSC's UK CRM practice. Stan is also working towards his PhD (part-time) studying the impact of online, interactive relationships upon the function and practice of marketing.

Previously, Stan held board-level positions for operating divisions of Unilever and Burson-Marsteller, world leaders in consumer goods and public relations respectively. He was also a global marketer with Cable & Wireless.

Stan Maklan co-authored *Competing on Value*, a best-selling management book that integrates key concepts associated with business process and brand management.

Email: smaklan@csc.com

Contents

List of figures

Cranfield School of Management Research Reports Series

The Cranfield School of Management Research Reports series is a major new initiative from Cranfield School of Management and Financial Times Prentice Hall.

The series combines the best in primary research from one of the world's foremost management schools with the traditional publishing and marketing skills of Financial Times Prentice Hall. The reports are designed to allow senior managers to apply the lessons from this research to their own organisations in order to promote best practice across a range of industries.

For further information on other titles in the series, please contact Financial Times Prentice Hall on + 44 (0)1704 508080.

Editorial board

Professor Alan Harrison, Professor of Operations and Logistics, Cranfield School of Management

Gill Marshall, Corporate Communications Manager, Cranfield School of Management

Professor Malcolm McDonald, Professor of Marketing Strategy and Deputy Director, Cranfield School of Management

Professor Susan Vinnicombe, Director of Graduate Research and Professor of Organisational Behaviour, Cranfield School of Management

Professor David Tranfield, Professor of Management, Director of Research and Deputy Director, Cranfield School of Management

Professor Shaun Tyson, Professor of Human Resource Management and Head of the Strategic Human Resources Group, Cranfield School of Management

Foreword

This is undoubtedly the most exciting period of my many years helping organisations maximise the business benefits from information technology. Traditionally, technology improved the process by which business operated through better accounting, decision support, engineering and manufacturing systems. Today, technology is profoundly affecting the everyday lives of everyone, in both their work and private lives. In the IT industry, we observe that the focus of our clients' investments is likewise moving from the 'back-office' to the 'front-office'.

Organisations find that changing their front-offices in response to the opportunities created by new technologies is a far different challenge than that faced with their back-office systems. Many of the familiar issues around managing change and leadership remain, but these are supplemented with the demands of individual customers who want it all, now, cost effectively and of very high quality. Some companies will have no choice but to allow customers a clear view into the deep recesses of their own organisations. This possibility raises interesting questions for senior managers in all industries: Will your ethics and practices meet society's expectations? Do your processes and quality control procedures, when fully visible, promote confidence in your ability to deliver? Do you really put customers first in your thinking?

The rate of change in technology advance at times outstrips companies' ability to understand its implications fully. The definitive book on becoming customer-centric has yet to be written; a body of well-accepted tools and methodologies is only now emerging. We observe that the business case for becoming a customer centric organisation is not always understood.

We have been working with a leading European business school that first published in the area of relationship marketing ten years ago: Cranfield University School of Management. Our association is adding to both our understanding of the online, interactive world and helping our consultants develop leading-edge methodologies and frameworks for our client engagements. We have sponsored an 18-month project to develop a well-grounded means of creating business cases that will help companies manage the substantial investments in CRM that they wish to make. We are happy to share with the wider business community the results of an early stage of this project in the form of this report, reviewing both academic and practitioner business case models, and their conceptual underpinnings.

Ronald W. Mackintosh
President and Chief Executive
European Group, Computer Sciences Corporation

Acknowledgements

The sponsorship of this research by CSC is gratefully acknowledged. The authors would also like to thank Andrew Myers and Dr David Smith for their contribution to the project, and Professor Malcolm McDonald and Merlin Stone for their comments.

Introduction

AIMS AND OBJECTIVES OF THE REPORT

This report presents the results of a major survey of the field of CRM, carried out by Cranfield School of Management with the assistance and sponsorship of CSC. The report aims to introduce and discuss six major topics currently being debated by academics and CRM practitioners. These six themes are:

- the explosion of interest in CRM and what CRM means – is technology necessary for CRM?;

- the business case for CRM and valuing customers;

- how to implement successful CRM projects;

- the components of CRM: Back-office and front-office systems;

- organisational and cultural implications of CRM;

- the likely future of CRM.

CRM systems require a highly participatory kind of programme management.

REPORT STRUCTURE

The structure of this report is driven by the key themes that emerged from the authors' review of the field of CRM literature. There has been an explosion of interest in CRM and the reasons for this are discussed in the first part of Chapter 1. It quickly became clear that Marketing people exhibited rather different attitudes and approaches to CRM from IT people and these are explored in the later sections of Chapter 1.

CRM systems require a highly participatory kind of programme management, one that delivers the systems that customers require on the day it 'goes live', rather than one that delivers against a contract written at the programme's inception. Management must allow customers 'into' the development of the new processes at a much earlier stage than normal, perhaps before it is even comfortable doing so. So, appropriate performance measurement systems that allow management to understand both the value the company creates for customers and the value that customers create for the company are needed to keep the value exchange in balance. These measures are discussed in more detail in Chapter 2. Chapter 3 is concerned with the implementation of CRM on a step on step basis, based on a customer-centric approach that involves detailed customer analysis and segmentation. Chapter 4 looks at CRM technology, and Chapter 5 considers some of the organisational and cultural issues that may arise during the implementation of CRM. Chapter 6 summarises the state of CRM to date and suggests possible future developments in CRM.

1

Investing in customers

There is no more vexing issue facing companies today than how they will relate to their customers in the emerging interactive, customer-focused environment.

Over the past twenty to thirty years, companies grappled with the question: 'In which product markets should we compete?' The other two domains of strategy, namely customer and channel, tended to occupy a slightly lower place in the pecking order of the strategic planning process.

Recently, the question managers have been asking is less about product market selection and more: 'in which of our customer segments should we invest, maintain or divest'? For many, the choice of which products and services to offer is made after there is agreement on customer development priorities. In effect, managers are now willing to let desirable customers influence, and in some cases determine, the company's product portfolio strategy.

Managers are now willing to let desirable customers influence, and in some cases determine, the company's product portfolio strategy.

This focus on customer strategy is linked to a number of trends that have come together coincidentally:

- new technologies make it possible to serve individual customers cost-effectively;

- the political mantra of the 1980s, choice plus customer sovereignty, has probably altered customer behaviour and attitudes to suppliers for ever;

- there is an increasingly rich and well-founded academic literature base supporting the notion that focusing on one-to-one relationships with customers versus traditional mass or niche marketing enhances corporate performance;

- companies that have successfully embraced Business Process Re-engineering have increased their operational capability to the point where they can better respond to individual customer needs.

As with so many emerging trends, there has been an explosion of jargon and acronyms, accompanied by a turf battle between academics, consultants, software/hardware vendors and even telecommunications firms for 'thought leadership' in this area of customer relationship management. Even the Post Office is entering the fray with its latest marketing campaign emphasising its ability in helping organisations improve customer management. With so many firms repositioning themselves in the market place, and with so many new firms entering, one might be excused for feeling a bit lost and confused.

Relationship marketing emphasises the benefits of retaining customers; loyal customers are known to be more profitable.

This report presents a summary review of the field of customer relationship management (CRM) and represents the outcome of a comprehensive database and library search covering books, journals and other publications. The authors have tracked practitioner and academic articles within the last decade, and relevant papers and reports from both worlds have been reviewed. Hundreds of items have been examined during the production of this report, which we believe to be the most comprehensive survey of the field of CRM to have been carried out to date.

It represents the first stage of a project funded by Computer Sciences Corporation (CSC) to deliver a methodology for helping companies determine the benefits from their investments in this area. While there is evidently not a fully defined business model available to the reader that can readily be adapted for use, a number of key themes have emerged during the review of academic and practitioner publications about CRM. These themes have been used as headings for this report.

1.1 THE EXPLOSION OF INTEREST IN CRM

The huge surge of interest in CRM seems to be attributable to the fact that it represents a practical way for organisations to implement relationship marketing. Relationship marketing emphasises the benefits of retaining customers; loyal customers are known to be more profitable. To implement relationship marketing successfully, companies have to know more about their customers. This means establishing two-way communication: from company to customer, and from customer to company. Both the requirement for increased information and the requirement for better means of communication are met by CRM, although it has been argued (Saunders, 1999) that CRM has already failed in these objectives. This is because most of its applications are pre-Internet technologies, and that a new model to synchronise cross-channel relationships, dubbed 'eRelationship management' or eRM, is required.

The authors' interest in CRM arises from a general interest in using IT for marketing applications. One of the authors was involved in a project to look at CRM and data warehousing in the financial services sector in 1998. Managing relationships in the CRM world requires an alignment of people, processes and technologies, and, unquestionably, new technologies are expected to play a vital role in the future in building customer relationships, as shown in Fig. 1.1.

Technology	1998	18 months previously
Internet (gathering customer data)	62%	6%
Electronic data interchange (EDI)	58%	9%
E-mail	54%	9%
Expect to have a data warehouse by 2002	83%	40%

FIGURE 1.1

Vitally important technology for communicating with customers

(*Source:* adapted from Economist Intelligence Unit (EIU), 1998)

According to a survey conducted at the end of 1998 by Softworld, 54 per cent of UK businesses claim to be able to target potential customers more effectively through the use of software systems in sales and marketing. Fifty-five per cent said they are planning to review their sales and marketing IT systems in 1999, with 33 per cent expecting to buy new systems and 22 per cent expecting to upgrade existing systems (Littlewood, 1999). Web sites have been set up by 70 per cent, and contact management packages, which allow navigation around basic 'name and address' databases, have been adopted by 47 per cent of businesses who are keen to automate paper-based contact management at a reasonably low cost (Littlewood, 1999). In an international survey, Ernst and Young found that companies had increased CRM spending by 31 per cent in a year when technology spending had levelled off to 8 per cent overall and that retaining customers was considered to be the most important CRM objective for 29 per cent, and the most important e-commerce objective for 27 per cent (Ernst and Young, 1999). The same survey found that the overall percentage of IT spend on e-commerce was set to double from 7 per cent in 1997 to 14 per cent in 2002. Thirty-nine per cent of respondents currently offered Internet transaction processing and 93 per cent expected to offer it by the end of 2002.

According to the Chartered Institute of Marketing survey, 48 per cent of sales and marketing departments use in-house marketing databases, which store information on potential customers and include data management and data mining functions for profiling and targeting customers. This figure is expected to grow to 73 per cent by the end of 2000. However, many departments are becoming more ambitious, and enterprise resource planning systems (ERP) are expected to become a fast-growing, technology-aiding market during the next three years. ERP is a back-office software system designed to manage resources efficiently across various areas of a business, including sales and marketing, human resources, finance and accounting, manufacturing systems and order entry. Only 13 per cent of firms used ERP at the end of 1998, but this is predicted to rise to 38 per cent by the end of 2000 (Littlewood, 1999).

1.2 THE ORIGINS OF CRM

CRM is a recent phenomenon and is rapidly becoming a major discipline in its own right. Its origins may be traced to the management of customer information first collected by the 'frequent flier' programmes of the 'high-fare' airlines in an attempt to stop defections to 'low-fare' carriers (Feldman, 1999). Between 1994 and 1997, spending on customer relationship management software and services, including customer service applications, grew from $200 million to $1.1 billion in the USA (Sweat and Hibbard, 1999). In 1998, the Economist Intelligence Unit (EIU), in conjunction with Andersen Consulting, published the results of a CRM survey of companies around the world. The study revealed a new, heightened focus on CRM as a discipline; a focus that is beginning to drive change in leading organisations (Economist Intelligence Unit, 1998). They found that companies are increasing their customer focus and using a process approach to customer relationship management. This represents a marked shift from the traditional transaction-based and functionally managed approach where the relationship with a customer is divided up between and dealt with by different departments.

This process approach seems to be an important characteristic of CRM. The EIU report also found that successful companies manage customer relationships based on potential profitability, with 75 per cent of respondents already segmenting and differentiating their treatment of customers. Customer profitability was expected to be the second most important customer-related performance measure in 2002, as shown in Fig. 1.2.

The results from this study and others indicate an increasing focus on the lifetime value of the customer, in line with the increased adoption of relationship marketing. For example, a survey by Abram Hawkes and Market Shape (Reed, 1997) found that 90 per cent of organisations recognise the value of customer retention. Sixty-one per cent thought there were links between customer loyalty and the duration of the customer relationship, and 45 per cent said that loyalty marketing yielded a better return on investment than expenditure on advertising. Even though the importance of CRM is recognised by companies, not all of them are acting on it. The same study found that only 45 per cent of respondent companies had a customer care programme.

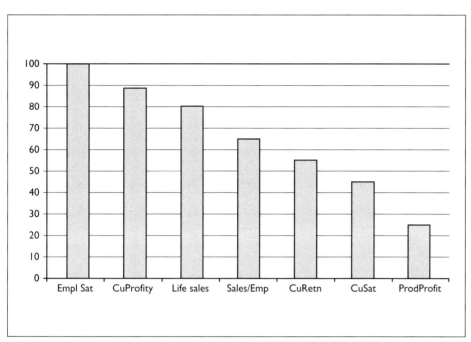

(*Source:* EIU, 1998)

FIGURE 1.2

Critically important customer-related performance measures in 2002

KEY TO TERMS

Empl Sat	Employee satisfaction
CuProfity	Customer profitability
Life sales	Lifetime sales
Sales/Emp	Sales per employee
CuRetn	Customer retention
CuSat	Customer satisfaction
ProdProfit	Product profitability

The results of the literature searches carried out for this report clearly indicate a growing interest in CRM. The tenor of much of the literature about CRM is that companies will have to adopt it to survive. Changes in the banking sector, driven by economic need and market competition, are a case in point. Axson (1992) traces developments in retail banking in the UK from 1981 to 1990: retail bank staff grew by 26 per cent, the number of ATMs increased by 476 per cent, the number of building societies was reduced from 253 to 99, and total bad debt provisions increased from £1.7 billion to £12.6 billion. Adolf and Hooda (1997) underline the point, discussing developments in the banking industry between 1980 and 1996:

> ... the banking industry drove down its ratio of operating expenses to net revenues from 66.1 per cent to 62.7 per cent, an improvement of 3.4 percentage points. During the same time period, however, the industry's share of financial institution assets fell from 36 per cent to 23 per cent – a decline of 13 percentage points.

CRM is a management approach that enables organisations to identify, attract and increase retention of profitable customers by managing relationships with them.

Numbers like these clearly indicate the mounting pressure in this sector. As Mitchell (1997) says, new entrants in financial services will be offering better service to customers. Nor do these new entrants have to carry the legacy of the past in terms of perceived inefficiency, poor service, and even mis-selling. The bank in your pocket might be called Virgin or be more famous for selling toothpaste; it may not even have any branches (Ratcliff, 1998). One such entrant into financial services is Intuit, the financial software company now offering desktop car insurance. This development has come about as a result of Intuit thinking about its role in the market place, rather than solely about the products it makes.

Still more dramatic are the developments in banking in North America since 1995, where online and telephone banking have resulted in major changes in customer behaviour. Even in 1995, only 56 per cent of US and 38 per cent of Canadian retail banking transactions were carried out in the branch; by 1998 the numbers were around 41 per cent and 21 per cent respectively (Darlington in Tapscott *et al.*, 1998). Changes of this magnitude suggest that CRM is central to survival for most organisations. 'Do nothing' or 'wait and see' are not viable options: 'CRM should be the center of your universe ... the best way to organize the information you use.' (Allen Bonde, analyst with the Extraprise Group, quoted in Colkin, 1999)

1.3 CRM: A DEFINITION

CRM is defined as 'a management approach that enables organisations to identify, attract and increase retention of profitable customers by managing relationships with them' (Ovum report quoted in Hobby, 1999). In other words, CRM is:

- about identifying, satisfying, retaining, and maximising the value of a company's best customers;

- a sales and service business strategy where the organisation wraps itself around the customer, so that whenever there is interaction, the message exchanged is appropriate for that customer; this means knowing all about that customer and what the profitability of that customer is going to be (Curley, 1999);

- an effort to create the whole picture of a given customer, bringing together consistent, comprehensive and credible information on all aspects of the existing relationship, such as profitability information, risk profiles and cross-sell potential (Papows, 1999).

CRM can be seen as an application of one-to-one marketing and relationship marketing, which means being willing and able to change your behaviour towards an individual customer based on what the customer tells you and what else you know about that customer (Peppers, Rogers and Dorf, 1999). It is essentially about using existing customer information to your company's advantage – and to improve customer service by avoiding the needless repetition of the same basic data (Couldwell, 1999).

Fletcher (1999) suggests that CRM is a way of using existing customer information and of controlling further data as it accumulates over time. CRM also means ensuring that staff on the front line have easy access to customer histories. This requires specialist software that links all parts of the business together and allows staff at all levels of the organisation to see up-to-the-minute customer information on a continuous basis.

Texts on relationship marketing also stress the importance of two-way communication, which is a feature of current CRM definitions, as is the focus on customer retention (Lockard, 1998; Deighton, 1996). The role of technology in enabling CRM is emphasised; Kutner and Cripps (1997) define CRM as 'data driven marketing'. Peppers and Rogers (1995) claim that, '… the marketplace of the future is undergoing a technology-driven metamorphosis'. This means that marketing and IT will have to work more closely together, and that organisations may have to restructure in order to maximise the return on their customer information.

> Customer relationship management is a combination of business process and technology that seeks to understand a company's customers from the perspective of who they are, what they do, and what they're like.
>
> (Couldwell, 1998)

The integration of the IT and marketing and service functions is highlighted by Galbreath (1998):

> Those activities an enterprise performs to identify, select, acquire, develop, and retain increasingly loyal and profitable customers. CRM integrates sales, marketing and service functions through business process automation, technology solutions and information resources to maximise each customer contact. CRM facilitates relationships among enterprises, their customers, business suppliers and employees.

A high level of information technology is not always a prerequisite for implementing the principles of CRM.

and by Kaplan, quoted in Fletcher (1999):

> ... data warehouses have tended to be owned by the IT department and database marketing is more for the sales force. CRM is a holistic approach to using customer information all over the company.

Harris, also quoted in Fletcher (1999), suggests that this is not an entirely new concept:

> Organisations have been managing customer relationships as well as they can for some time. What is new is the fact that software is now available that links the whole company together to manage customers.

Nevertheless, a high level of information technology is not always a prerequisite for implementing the principles of CRM, and it has been argued that people and processes are more important to service delivery than technology (McKean, 1999). A profitable, mid-sized South American bank, recognising that they could wait indefinitely for a perfect IT system, used their existing modest systems to forward their limited customer information to the front-line sales and service people who, in turn, fed back any further information that they had gained about customers. Thus, information was gathered and managed by sales people, rather than by surveying customers or electronically interrogating and managing a database (Hall, 1999).

Kutner and Cripps (1997) say that CRM is founded on four tenets:

1. customers should be managed as important assets;

2. customer profitability varies – not all customers are equally desirable;

3. customers vary in their needs, preferences, buying behaviour and price sensitivity;

4. by understanding customer drivers and customer profitability, companies can tailor their offerings to maximise the overall value of their customer portfolio.

According to Sophron Partners, a comprehensive CRM system comprises four main technology components (Curley, 1999):

- a data warehouse with customer, contract, transaction and channel data

- analysis tools to examine the database and identify customer behaviour patterns

- campaign management tools to allow the marketing department to define communications and facilitate automatic generation of those communications

- interfaces to the operational environment to maintain the marketing database and communications channels to deliver the messages.

So, CRM is a framework or discipline, rather than a product (Couldwell, 1999). Anton (1996) sees CRM as an integrated approach to managing relationships, requiring continuous improvement. This is illustrated in Fig. 1.3.

Irrespective of the definition of CRM, companies are embracing it as a strategic activity. A survey among fifty blue-chip organisations, published by Chordiant software company in 1999, showed that over 80 per cent of respondents felt that CRM was 'very important' or 'critical' in determining the future success of their companies, and that 75 per cent felt that technology was the most effective weapon that a company has at its disposal for implementing CRM (Fletcher, 1999).

FIGURE 1.3

CRM across multiple markets

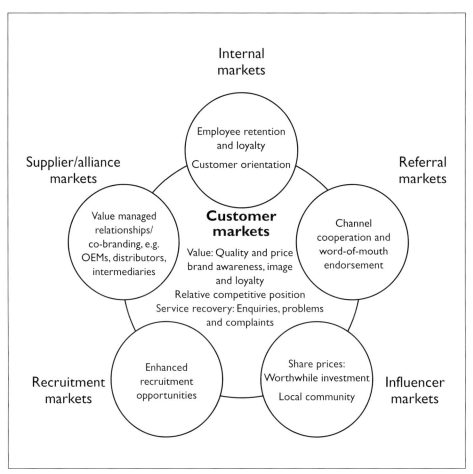

Internal
markets

Employee retention
and loyalty

Customer orientation

Supplier/alliance
markets

Referral
markets

Value managed
relationships/
co-branding, e.g.
OEMs, distributors,
intermediaries

**Customer
markets**

Channel
cooperation and
word-of-mouth
endorsement

Value: Quality and price
brand awareness, image
and loyalty
Relative competitive position
Service recovery: Enquiries, problems
and complaints

Recruitment
markets

Enhanced
recruitment
opportunities

Share prices:
Worthwhile investment

Local community

Influencer
markets

(*Source:* adapted from Cranfield's multiple markets model)

1.4 THE CATALYSTS FOR CRM

CRM has come about partly as a result of the emergence of relationship marketing and a focus on customer retention. Research indicating that retaining customers is more profitable than acquiring new ones has supported this development. The work by Bain, quoted in Reichheld (1996), is of particular interest, as it covers a number of studies in various industries, which demonstrate that retained customers are more profitable. Bain's findings indicate that a 5 per cent increase in customer retention results in an increase in average lifetime value of between 35 per cent and 95 per cent. Some of the industries mentioned – and the improvement in customer lifetime value – are software (35 per cent), office building management (40 per cent), credit card (75 per cent), publishing (85 per cent), and an advertising agency (95 per cent). The profit impact of this loyalty effect is illustrated in Fig. 1.4.

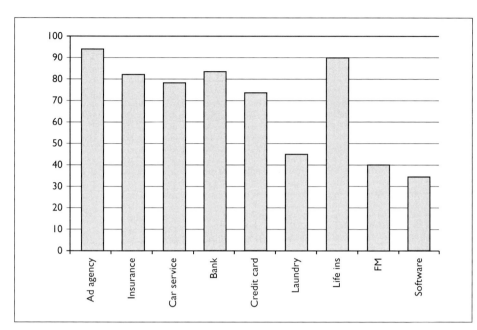

FIGURE 1.4

Impact of a 5 per cent increase in retention rate on customer net present value

(*Source:* adapted from Reichheld, 1996)

Loyal customers are more profitable. In the case of the advertising industry, an analysis of five agencies shows a match between annual customer revenue retention and productivity. In insurance broking, the figures from six brokers demonstrate a correlation between customer retention and pre-tax profit margin. There are six reasons why loyal customers are more profitable (Reichheld, 1996):

1. Customer acquisition costs may be high, so customers may not become profitable unless they are retained for one or more years.

2. There will be a stream of profits from the customer in each year after acquisition costs are covered.

3. Customers buy more over time, so revenues go up. This finding is also supported by Hughes's work on a loyalty programme in a car rental company that resulted in retention rates doubling (from 40 per cent to 80 per cent), plus a dramatic increase in year by year spending (techguide.com, 1998). By year 3 of the loyalty programme, average customer spending had more than tripled over its pre-programme level.

4. Companies become more efficient at serving them (there is a learning curve to the relationship), so costs go down.

5. Retained and satisfied customers may refer other potential customers.

6. The relationship has a value to the customer too, and so retained customers tend to become less price-sensitive. Brand loyalty also reduces price sensitivity; companies with a higher proportion of their spending on sales promotion activities, which are often price-based,

have a lower Return on Investment (ROI) than companies who concentrate more of their spending on advertising and brand building (Hallberg 1995).

However, customer loyalty is diminishing and customer defection is a growing problem. An example quoted by Reeves (1998) from the mobile telephone industry makes the point that churn in that industry has reached 'epidemic' proportions, averaging 25 per cent per annum in Europe and 30 per cent in the USA. The picture in financial services is similar: some sectors of the insurance industry face 35 per cent of their customers allowing their policies lapse each year (Curley, 1999).

Information-intensive markets require information-intensive strategies and that information should be organised into a database which would then become the organisation's core asset.

In managing this tension between rising customer churn and the growing recognition that retained customers are more profitable, the role of marketing and IT is key. Glazer (1997) discusses the sudden emergence of information as an issue, and suggests that one reason for this may be that new technologies are making data much more visible, thereby forcing a re-evaluation of underlying assumptions. He argues that information-intensive markets require information-intensive strategies and that information should be organised into a Customer Information File or database which would then become the organisation's core asset.

Arguably, this is rather an IT-driven view. A different perspective has been suggested by a number of commentators who view customers – not the information database – as a company's core asset. The information database then becomes the means to exploit that asset. Schmittlein (1995), for example, views the creation of a customer database as merely the start of a process of managing the customer as a strategic asset; the customer will be managed via database marketing, e-commerce, and loyalty programmes. The outcomes will be greater focus in the development of new products and a more loyal customer base.

This is a significant shift: from a product focus where the effort is directed towards selling products to as many customers as possible, to a customer focus where the aim is to provide a customer with as many products and services as possible (Peppers and Rogers, 1998). Marketing success is measured by share of customer spend, not by market share (Peppers and Rogers, 1995). This customer focus is expected to have an impact not just on the ways that organisations view their customers and how they treat them, but also on how companies organise themselves and how they measure success. A survey by the EIU found a major shift was occurring in organising around customer types, which was expected to rise from 18 per cent of companies surveyed to 50 per cent by 2002. Seventy per cent of respondents expected to switch to CRM during the next five years, and three-quarters expected to report a high degree of integration between sales and IT functions over this time (as opposed to one-quarter today). As far as measurement is concerned, there have been big shifts in the number of companies tracking customer retention and customer profitability. To enable these changes, the number of companies having a data warehouse is expected to more than double to 83 per cent by 2002 (EIU, 1998).

Although CRM seems to offer a way of reversing the shift towards commoditisation, identifying customers who are susceptible to relationships may not be easy (*American Banker*, 1998). Even when identified, the privacy of these customers has to be respected. Banks and insurance companies head the list of companies for which consumers say that privacy is 'very important' (Culnan, 1995). Ethical policies on the use of customer information will need to be developed if information-intensive strategies are not to rebound on themselves.

Acceptance of CRM is by no means universal.

Acceptance of CRM is by no means universal. Woods and Remondi (1996) find that many high-technology companies are still using outdated marketing approaches, and are not recognising the potential benefits to sales effectiveness and long-term marketing success. Others think that classical marketing skills, and the basics of quality, cost and convenience, rather than 'expensive IT and neural networks', are what is needed to give an organisation a competitive edge (Hagel *et al.*, 1996). A third view is that there is a choice – that companies can *either* focus on being product manufacturers, providing an array of different products sold through a variety of channels *or* aspire to become relationship managers, developing long-term, multi-product relationships with their customers, even though some of their products might be sourced from third parties (Power and Douglas, 1997).

1.5 THE MARKETING PERSPECTIVE

The marketing perspective on CRM focuses on its potential to offer better customer service and to improve marketing effectiveness through better focus (McDonald and Wilson, 1999; Bessen, 1993). Berkley and Gupta (1994) list a number of ways in which customer service can be improved through IT, including reliability, security, efficiency and communication, as well as quality control and service monitoring. It is argued that this will also lead to better long-term profitability.

So who benefits from CRM? Technology offers the opportunity to capture information and understand the impact of advertising on purchase behaviour, potentially in real time (Hagel and Sacconaghi, 1996). The customer information file enables better matching of marketing offers to prospects (Harrison, 1993), as well as tracking the effectiveness of marketing programmes (Mann, 1990) and providing the basis for future planning (Shani and Chalasani, 1993). All these factors are benefits to the organisation. However, customers can benefit as well when product and/or service offers are better targeted to the individual or segment; tailoring offers to customers' individual needs can result in more loyal customers (Mitchell, 1998).

CRM systems are seen to offer operational improvements (Stein and Caldwell, 1998) and long-term success through longer and closer relationships (Beckett-Camarata *et al.*, 1998). In addition, customer data analysis enables organisations to identify the customers it does *not* want to have. The 80:20 rule suggests that 80 per cent of profits are generated by 20 per cent of customers, but some banks have found even more extreme differences:

> Some commercial banks have found that 10 per cent of their current account customers are responsible for more than 100 per cent of their profits (i.e. the other 90 per cent are, on average, loss-making).
>
> (Stone *et al.*, 1996)

Similarly, studies in the telecommunications industry have shown that 80 per cent of profits can come from as few as 3 per cent of the buildings in a company's territory (Computer Sciences Corporation, 1998).

On the other hand, a customer-centred view recognises that, as customers often take time to develop a mature relationship, there may be temporary loss-leaders for some products. Such customers may not be immediately profitable but, if sufficient is known about them through research and accumulated data, they may be worth retaining, should they join a profitable market segment in the future (Kiesnoski, 1999).

Case study • CITIBANK

Citibank made extensive offerings to the credit card market for college students; for many students it was the only card they could obtain. The loyalty that ensued from this approach paid off: many of those former students have remained with Citibank because it issued their first credit card (Kiesnoski, 1999).

From a marketing perspective, CRM is not yet well developed in many organisations. According to a benchmarking survey by QCi Assessment, company performance on a range of relationship marketing measures, from analysis and planning through to customer management activity and measuring the effect, scores less than 40 out of a possible 100 points (Gamble *et al.*, 1999).

Information technology has the potential to transform marketing by generating market knowledge, supporting group decision-making, and facilitating customer transactions.

1.6 THE IT PERSPECTIVE

The IT perspective is that these changes are happening anyway, and are being driven by evolving customer demands (Schultz, 1993) and the development of enabling technologies. Landberg believes that this results in a three-stage evolution in customer management strategy in the financial services industry. In the first phase the emphasis is on cross-selling; in the second, on additional product or distribution capability; and in the third, on value added services (Landberg, 1998). A move to one-to-one marketing with the final customer is seen as an inevitable consequence of customer demands and new technologies; therefore, organisations will have to integrate their marketing and communications (Schultz, 1996). One result will be the increased visibility of the 'digital group' (Parsons, Zeisser and Waitman, 1996) and a greater need to manage organisational interdependencies.

Several authors comment that IT can be either a bridge to serving customers better when used properly or a barrier if not. A key barrier to the successful deployment of IT can be attitudinal (Domegan, 1996; Stone *et al.*, 1993). However, information technology has the potential to transform marketing by generating market knowledge, supporting group decision-making, and facilitating customer transactions (*Management Today*, 1994). The financial services industry recognises the importance of the strategic use of IT for exploring markets and providing a competitive edge, according to a survey of 80 major insurance firms reported by Codington and Wilson (1994).

Most financial services companies now have some form of customer marketing database. However, these do not always perform well in supporting customer management (Naval, 1998; *Insurance Systems Bulletin*, 1993). Two things are required: properly managed IT, and a strategic approach to the use and integration of IT systems within the business (McDonald and Wilson, 1999; Haapaniemi, 1996; Tavinen, 1995). The message that the implementation of relationship marketing is a strategic issue is strongly supported in the literature (see, for example, Economist Intelligence Unit, 1998; Fletcher and Wright, 1996; Perrien *et al.*, 1993).

An important element in approaching CRM strategically is the application of customer segmentation; identifying much more clearly which customers are desirable and which are not. IBM, for example, has developed a highly successful telesales operation which dealt with 300 000 customers and generated more than US$4 billion in 1995. The steps that IBM followed were to develop its understanding of its customer's business, improve its customer segmentation, and treat sales and marketing as a process (Stevens, 1996).

Cravens *et al.* (1998) describe a process of mapping the route to strategic leadership by which companies such as Dell, Virgin and Boeing are able to match market opportunities to organisation capabilities. They argue that:

> There is increasing evidence from successful companies, that distinctive competencies are a combination of the organisation's assets and skills (e.g., innovation), which are employed in achieving the desired outcomes (e.g., new products) through the essential processes of the business. Competitive advantage results from processes that yield superior customer value.

The development of an effective CRM strategy constitutes an essential building block for the integration of these business processes and systems.

1.7 DEVELOPING A CRM STRATEGY AND CRM ARCHITECTURE

Those charged with developing a CRM strategy can learn much from earlier corporate change initiatives, such as TQM (Total Quality Management), BPR (Business Process Re-engineering) and ERP (Enterprise Resource Planning).

On the one hand, CRM can be regarded as just another change programme. The literature suggests that it requires the same level of company support and alignment as its antecedents, namely:

- strong executive sponsorship

- middle management alignment

- alignment of rewards and measures to the desired new behaviours

- integration of business systems towards a common goal

- programme management to maintain energy and progress, and to overcome barriers

- new information systems to support new business processes

- mass involvement and education efforts with employees and suppliers.

The key stakeholder in the change programme, the customer, is not under the company's direct control.

On the other hand, CRM is very different from many of its antecedents that have dealt principally with back-office and internal processes. While the success factors listed above are still necessary, they are not sufficient. Front-office change offers additional challenges:

- the key stakeholder in the change programme, the customer, is not under the company's direct control;

- competitive offers, the result of competitors' own CRM programmes, are also visible to the customer.

- it is hard to pilot and carefully roll out new systems and processes – often these immediately enter the public domain and are subject to intense scrutiny from launch;

- a back-office system that is delayed or fails to perform initially has a financial cost, but does not automatically lead to lost business. A front-office system that fails may drive away some of your best customers, many of whom will never return.

In this chapter we conclude that CRM covers a broad range of technologies and solutions. We argue that new technologies or 'point solutions' do not constitute a CRM programme. These technologies, processes and new people skills need to be integrated into an overall architecture (see Fig. 1.5) that enables the company to move from a 'make and sell' approach to one that is characterised by 'listen and serve'.

We will use Fig. 1.5 as a 'road map' throughout the report, to indicate which aspect of CRM is to be explored in each section. As shown, the 'listen and serve' architecture pulls together the following areas of technology solutions:

FIGURE 1.5

CRM architecture

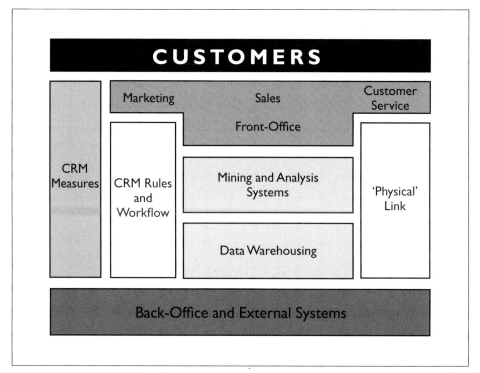

(*Source*: Stan Maklan, CSC, 1999b)

- The integrated front-office that provides any customer-facing person, be they in marketing, sales or customer service, with the full picture of the individual customer's needs, preferences and importance to the company. The technologies explored in Chapter 4 cover call centres, sales force automation and the Internet.

- A business intelligence system that learns on the basis of these interactions as well as from external data. The report suggests that business intelligence is further divided between data warehousing and data mining/analysis technologies. The warehousing technologies act as an information factory, gathering and preparing information for use by the business. Mining and analysis tools allow business users to understand how different customers differ in behaviour, motivation, cost and profitability. In Chapter 4 we also consider the back-office systems that are the key components of a CRM strategy.

- Workflow and business rules transmit business intelligence to the integrated front-office. On the basis of this learning, front-office employees are given powerful customer insights at the point of customer contact. They are also given guidelines and rules with which to understand how far they can go in satisfying customer requests. These rules empower front-office people to solve customer problems at the point of contact. The organisational and cultural implications of CRM developments are considered in Chapter 5.

- Finally, physical links to back-office systems permit this intelligent front-office to reach deep into its company's fulfilment systems so that the front-office can make sales and service promises based on the latest knowledge about what and when the company can deliver. A real-time, interactive front- and back-office conversation is considered best practice in CRM.

To talk meaningfully of embracing CRM is to accept a high level of corporate ambition.

1.8 A CRM PRACTITIONER'S VIEWPOINT

It is clear from this report that leading practitioners and academics take a very broad view of the definition of customer relationship management. CRM's object is to align corporate attention and investment among the most promising customers in terms of financial return. Its strategy is to engage the customer in an interactive dialogue that enables the company to create exactly what the customer wants and is willing to pay for. Its scope embraces relationships with customers, employees and suppliers, and touches all aspects of internal corporate processes and structures.

To talk meaningfully of embracing CRM is to accept a high level of corporate ambition, which for many means a large change programme to shift the corporate focus from product to customer. Of course, less far-reaching investment programmes in customer management can still prove worthwhile for most companies since there is no a priori need for managers to pursue the goal of ever-larger programmes.

It might be useful at this point for managers to audit their own organisation's CRM strategy. In section 1.9, we consider the degree to which CRM can be adopted in an organisation by providing a self-completion questionnaire to qualify the ambitions of your own company.

1.9 EXERCISE: AUDIT YOUR CRM STRATEGY

CRM in your organisation

Against each question, tick one box on the right according to how strongly you agree or disagree.

	disagree strongly	disagree	neither agree nor disagree	agree	agree strongly
1. We have a clear understanding of how our customers' needs differ from each other and how their potential contribution to our company differs between them.	☐	☐	☐	☐	☐
2. We will, at least in the very near future, make the products and offer the services demanded by our best customers irrespective of our own product plans.	☐	☐	☐	☐	☐
3. We will sell and service our customers directly if that is their wish even at the risk of upsetting long-standing relationships with distributors, retailers and other third parties.	☐	☐	☐	☐	☐
4. We are building (have built) systems and processes to enable us to manage the entire customer experience with our organisation from first enquiry to solving ongoing problems related to our products and services.	☐	☐	☐	☐	☐
5. We are building (have built) management information systems that enable us to understand the contribution to our profitability made by individual customers. On the basis of this information, we empower and measure our managers' ability to manage the customer base.	☐	☐	☐	☐	☐
Now score each tick as shown:	1	2	3	4	5
Enter your score per column in each box	☐	☐	☐	☐	☐

Total score:

How does your organisation score?

Score 0–9

Your organisation remains focused upon its own product/market strategy or operational effectiveness, rather than customising its offer for different customers or segments of customers.

This may be a successful strategy for your organisation if some of the following conditions are present:

- there is little apparent means of differentiating customer need and cost is the prime determinant of customer value;

- customer needs can be differentiated, but your organisation has opted for a strategy other than one that is customer-centric. This could be low-cost provider or at the other extreme, value-added branding such as Nike or Gap;

- the markets in which you are competing are supply limited and the priority is on pure operational considerations. This may happen if, for example, you offer systems implementation in an emerging software area that is chronically short of quality people, hold special Government licences or are entering a developing market.

Score 10–18

Your organisation is probably increasingly customer-focused in its strategy. Customer and competitive pressures are generating the need for increased flexibility in handling customer requests, there is real differentiation in how customers are managed and customer input is increasingly sought for important decisions.

This may be a transition stage while the organisation becomes truly customer directed. Experience suggests a number of tensions in this middle stage that managers need to resolve:

- it is difficult to quantify new business opportunities that are not grounded in new products or services;

- the leaders of the company have a more intuitive feel for the operational and product drivers that built the organisation than for what constitutes a truly customer-oriented business;

- irrespective of focus, it is not evident that the organisation has competencies in many of the value added areas demanded by customers;

- the customer information needed by customer-facing staff is not readily available.

Score 19–25

Your organisation has made a transition from 'make and sell' to 'listen and serve' or perhaps it was built that way from its inception.

There are different offers for different customers aligned to a clear understanding of customer profitability. Investment is allocated to its best return in terms of customer, and the business case for CRM is understood in terms of its impact on the value of the customer to the organisation.

In the next chapter, we look at how the business case for CRM can be supported, based on a customer-centric approach which points towards improvements in customer service, profitability and performance, and measures for the ROI on the systems themselves.

2

The business case for CRM

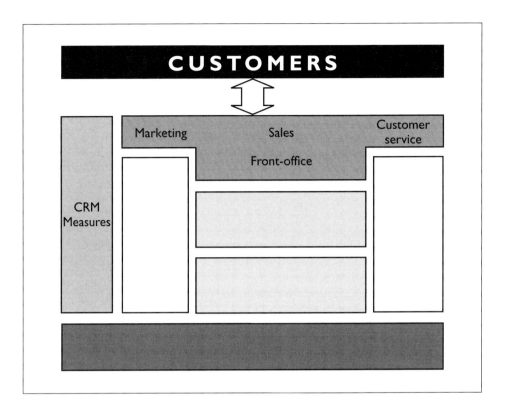

The value of the CRM software market is already substantial and growing fast, although it is difficult to arrive at precise figures. An estimate by the Yankee Group puts the market in integrated CRM systems (Enterprise Customer Management) at US$4.5 billion in 2000 (techguide.com, 1998), up from US$2.4 billion in 1998. Dataquest puts the market at $2 billion at the end of 1998 in the USA alone, rising to $3.5 billion by 2001 (Vijayan, 1998).

The various components of CRM are also marketed individually: customer support, help desk, SFA and other functions sold as point products or suites were said to be worth US$740 million in 1996 and growing at 40 per cent per annum (International Data Corp, cited in Stein, 1997).

Part of the market for CRM capability will be served by ERP add-ons. The ERP market is worth some US$500 million today and is forecast by Merrill Lynch to grow to US$8 billion by 2002 (Stein and Caldwell, 1998). ERP systems are increasingly built with CRM capabilities added on.

Financial services seem to be one of the more advanced industry sectors in CRM and some figures for CRM spending are available. Andersen Consulting, in a study for Hewlett-Packard, projected 1997–8 spending on relationship management in the USA financial services industry as US$600 million by retail financial markets, US$900 million by the retail insurance industry, and US$1.5 billion by retail banks. This gives a total of US$3 billion, spent mainly on data warehousing (Orenstein, 1997).

2.1 HOW THE BUSINESS CASE HAS BEEN SUPPORTED

In terms of new product revenues, the adopters of CRM exceeded their targets by almost twice that of manufacturers without customer-centred strategies.

There is very little hard evidence as to what the business case is for CRM, but there is widespread belief that CRM is vital for the future of many businesses. For example, the Chief Information Officer of Farmers Group Inc., the US insurer, says of CRM: 'The technology is ready, and the business case is overwhelming.' For the insurers, the business case revolves around identifying and retaining their most profitable customers. However, this can be problematic where the relationship is at arm's length through a financial intermediary (Curley, 1999). Another view of the business case for CRM comes from a survey of more than nine hundred executives across various manufacturing industries in Canada, undertaken by Deloitte Consulting. Their survey revealed that manufacturers who had adopted a CRM strategy exceeded their targets for sales growth by 65 per cent on average, whereas companies without such plans exceeded their targets by only about 17 per cent. In terms of new product revenues, the adopters of CRM exceeded their targets by more than 60 per cent, which was almost twice that of manufacturers without customer-centred strategies (Saunders, 1999).

There are only three simple rules for ensuring the success of customer relationship marketing. Measure, measure and measure.

However, there are some indications that CRM investments are failing to deliver or that possibly customer expectations are increasing faster than the ability of companies to keep up. Although spending in the USA on customer relationship management software, services and customer-service applications grew from $200 million to $1.1 billion between 1994 and 1997, the American Customer Satisfaction Index (ACSI) fell from 74 to 70 (on a point scale of 1 to 100) during the same period. (ACSI is a measure of consumer attitudes towards some 200 companies in 35 industries based on an annual survey conducted by the University of Michigan Business School, the American Society for Quality, and Arthur Andersen.) The index regained more than one point in 1998 but dropped again in the first quarter of 1999. While ACSI scores have improved for some companies and industries, customer satisfaction overall is not keeping pace with spending on customer-oriented technology (Sweat and Hibbard, 1999). As Gamble *et al.* (1999) comment:

> There are only three simple rules for ensuring the success of customer relationship marketing. Measure, measure and measure.

Yet, although CRM projects represent a major investment for most companies, many companies fail to measure the returns on their CRM systems. As well as the operational benefits of improved customer satisfaction and company performance, CRM systems can boost productivity and improve efficiency (Hall, 1997). Moreover, organisations sometimes focus on the hardware and software costs of such investments without realising the potentially significant costs of time, training and so forth (Rountree, 1997). Sometimes the benefits will be difficult or impossible to assess using traditional accounting measures – Goebel *et al.* (1998) discuss the usefulness of Activity-Based Costing (ABC) to marketers in assessing costs versus benefits of various activities. A general application of ABC to a company is described in Krupnicki and Tyson (1997). The application of ABC to customer profitability analysis is mentioned in Partridge and Perren (1998) and Sharman (1996).

The review of current writings about CRM suggests that the business case for CRM can be considered under four headings:

- improvements in customer service, satisfaction and retention
- increases in customer profitability
- changes in overall company profitability and performance
- the return on investment on CRM systems themselves.

Each of these aspects is now discussed in turn.

2.2 CUSTOMER SERVICE, SATISFACTION AND RETENTION

CRM systems offer the potential to modernise relationships in five vital ways: product customisation, tailored service, focusing on whole relationships and on customer lifetime value, and establishing multi-channel capabilities (Adolf and Hooda, 1997). This should result in better customer service, leading to increased satisfaction and loyalty. However, in order to turn this potential into profitable marketing decisions, organisations need to segment their customer database and target those segments most likely to respond to improved service offers.

Sometimes improving the service offer involves using new technology to increase access to a company's products or services. This has been particularly important in the financial services industry. Insurance companies, banks and brokerage houses are keen to realise the benefits of CRM through call centres or the Web by trying to provide the most accommodating environments possible to please their customers and to eliminate expensive customer turnover, which can cost as much as $400 per customer replaced (Hoard, 1999). Positive management of customer retention can yield major benefits; one financial services organisation increased renewal rates by 45 per cent and added £5.6 million to its bottom line by identifying potential lapsers and targeting them through the company's call centre (Roscoe, 1999).

The data warehouses used to support CRM can also help reduce customer turnover by providing 'early warning' signals. Hiss (1999) cites research showing that there is a great difference in behaviour between customers who say they are 'very satisfied' and those who say they are 'satisfied'; the very satisfied customers are six times more likely to repurchase than the merely satisfied customers. Improving repurchase behaviour or quantity is a tangible measure of the payback on increasing customer satisfaction.

Customer satisfaction is a key issue at AT&T's Universal Card.

Case study ● AT&T UNIVERSAL CARD

AT&T Universal Card have realised that anticipating future customer needs is just as important as satisfying current needs. Such needs are captured through focus groups, one-to-one interviews and customer surveys. The company reviews customer needs and attitudes on a regular basis. They even have a Director of Customer Listening whose job it is to communicate customer views to senior management. Some issues can be dealt with on a daily basis; others are reviewed at the end of a month and are then acted upon.

Although customer service and satisfaction are important measures of CRM, leading organisations are focusing on share of customer spend, as Peppers and Rogers (1995) suggest:

> ... focusing on share of customer spend, instead of overall market share, is probably the least expensive and most cost-efficient means of increasing overall sales – and, incidentally, market share.

It turns out that a small proportion of customers account for a large proportion of turnover and hence profit. In packaged and soft goods, 33 per cent of buying category accounts for at least 67 per cent of volume; this is the high-profit segment. Similarly, just 21 per cent of filmgoers account for 80 per cent of cinema attendance; and a Coca-Cola sponsored survey found that the top third of grocery shoppers were responsible for 80 per cent of grocery spending in a supermarket. Kraft foods found a similar pattern; across all their brands, the top third of households accounted for almost 70 per cent of the company's sales volume. In some categories the split is even more extreme; in yogurt, the top 16 per cent of households delivered 83 per cent of the volume, and for Diet Coke, 84 per cent of volume comes from just 8 per cent of households. This volume picture was also reflected in the profit from each segment; higher spend segments were more profitable (Hallberg, 1995).

Hiss (1999) also points out that customer profitability is not the only measure that should be considered. He underlines the importance of referenceability:

It may, be worthwhile to take on unprofitable or less profitable customers for the referenceability benefits.

> You may have to give up some profit to get a big-name company's business, but what if getting it means that you can finally close sales with two or three companies? That initial loss in profit becomes a great investment.

It may, therefore, be worthwhile in some cases to take on unprofitable or less profitable customers for the referenceability benefits. It is the potential value creation throughout the relationship lifetime that is the true measure of CRM.

2.3 INCREASES IN CUSTOMER PROFITABILITY

Grant and Schlesinger (1995) make a strong case for customer profitability measurement and management, arguing that:

> Companies embracing the principles of value exchange are operating on an entirely new playing field ... they define their target customer base, quantify the current and full-potential value of these relationships, and commit the entire company to closing the gap between the two.

This introduces the idea of segmenting the market and prioritising the most attractive customers, and excluding low-margin, low-profit customers from the outset (Peppers and Rogers, 1998; Reed, 1997). Segmentation permits more targeted marketing and the development of tailored products and service propositions, leading to customer retention (*American Banker*, 1995).

This approach is supported by Storbacka's findings that retrospective analysis of the customer base for profitability is a good basis for segmentation. Storbacka (1997) analysed the customer base of two banks, and found links between the value of the balance held, the customer lifetime and customer profitability.

Determining customer profitability will probably involve the use of Activity-Based Costing (ABC); simple cost allocation by volume can be seriously misleading. Crookes Healthcare, which makes over-the-counter healthcare products (e.g. Nurofen and Strepsils) and supplies chemists chains, wholesalers and grocery retailers, found a 600 per cent variation in costs of distribution between its customers, depending on their delivery requirements (Connolly and Ashworth, 1994). It is the 'pocket price' – the amount the seller actually realises from the sale – that is key. Invoice prices do not reflect payment terms, claims records or delivery charges, items that are specific to the customer and which can have a major impact on profitability. The construction of a customer database is usually the first step in identifying the pocket price (Schorsch, 1994).

Single period customer profitability analysis can, however, prove seriously misleading as a guide to marketing strategies (Carroll and Tadikonda, 1997). More important than short-term profit is the lifetime value of the customer. However, calculating the potential value of a customer is not straightforward, particularly where closely substitutable products exist. Reeves (1998) uses the example of the mobile telephone industry to make the point that technology convergence means that, to calculate the total lifetime value of a mobile telephone user, ordinary telephone use, Internet, and digital TV usage should be included.

Campbell and Cunningham (1990, in Ford, 1990) suggest a three-stage process for analysing customer profitability in business to business markets: life cycle classification, growth rate of customer's own demand, and relative share of customer's purchases. Focusing on the customers with the best long-term profit potential involves identifying profitable customer groups, analysing the way they use products, developing marketing programmes targeted specifically at them, and checking that they are satisfied (Duboff, 1992). The importance of identifying profitable customers is stressed by Wayland and Cole (1994): they liken it to Ted Williams' advice on achieving a high batting average: 'First, get a good pitch to hit.' One consequence of this selection process is that companies may have to begin discouraging certain types of less profitable customers; across-the-board retention programmes may be economically indefensible (Wayland and Cole, 1994).

Dorman and Hasan (1996) argue that, contrary to popular belief within the banking industry, banks do have many unprofitable customers. They mention research showing that a quarter of new customers each year for American banks never generate enough revenue to offset basic acquisition costs, and an additional 30 per cent never generate enough income to make a positive contribution to profits. They report the results of a customer profiling and targeting exercise by a retail bank: direct mail campaign costs fell by a third, yet response rates doubled. Also, the number of new accounts increased by 33 per cent and the profitability of new accounts by 32 per cent; defection rates fell 5 per cent; and lifetime value of customers grew by an estimated 20 per cent. Surprisingly, most banks are not doing effective database-driven targeted marketing; Rosenthal and McEachern (1997) claim research shows only one in eight banks adopt targeted marketing using an enterprise-wide strategy. U.S. Bank has recently changed the way it views customers and now scans all of its customers for value, risk, attrition, and propensity to buy (Heasley and Gross, 1997). Banco Central Hispano uses its CRM system to identify propensity to purchase; the response rate from mailings using this criterion is almost six times greater than the traditional mailshot (Forsyth, 1999).

McKean (1999) suggests that significant payback may be achieved on CRM investments not just through enhancing customer profitability, but also through identifying which customers are unlikely to pay their bills, which are more likely to commit fraud, and the likelihood of defection. Bennett (1992) claims that 25 per cent of the customers of service firms are ready to switch if a reasonable alternative becomes available. He suggests that the costs of customer disloyalty include not just the revenue foregone but the revenue lost from other customers as a result of negative word of mouth, the costs of replacing lost customers, and the costs and time spent recovering the company's position with dissatisfied customers.

Service leaders perform significantly better than the competition, with growth that is twice as fast, supported by price premiums and a much higher return on sales.

Grant and Schlesinger (1995) report on the use of a customer information database at AT&T. In 1994, AT&T attracted more than 1.2 million accounts while reducing acquisition costs by more than US$3 per customer; 50 per cent of the dollars invested in acquiring new customers led to a customer acquisition, as opposed to 5 per cent in 1990.

Most companies, however, are not able to measure the payback on CRM in this way. The Ernst and Young report (1999) found that, although 20 per cent of respondents said that the profitability of individual customers had increased since the introduction of CRM, over 60 per cent did not know what had happened to customer profitability as a result of CRM. However, two-thirds of respondents in the same survey claimed that CRM had been successful in encouraging cross-selling.

2.4 CHANGES IN OVERALL COMPANY PROFITABILITY AND PERFORMANCE

Research sponsored by Mosaic (techguide.com, 1998) claims that service leaders perform significantly better than the competition, with growth that is twice as fast, supported by price premiums and a much higher return on sales.

Grant and Schlesinger (1995) cite several examples of potential and actual performance improvements based on CRM. A Canadian grocery store, for example, discovered that it could increase future gross profits by 300 per cent if it expanded its customer base by 2 per cent, reduced defection rates by 5 per cent, and substituted two own-brand items for two branded purchases per customer visit. Taco Bell found that 30 per cent of its customer base accounted for more than 70 per cent of volume and focused on these customers; sales increased from US$1.6 billion in 1988 to US$4.5 billion in 1994. Earnings increased more than 300 per cent over the same period. Similar potential has been found in the retail banking sector. One such bank found that it could generate an incremental US$25 million after tax over three years by cross-selling each customer an additional 1.5 products (*American Banker*, 1998). Dell Computers is the arch-exponent of analysing its customer base to improve service and thereby generate significant market share gains.

Case study • DELL COMPUTERS

Dell, using an entirely telephone-based sales and service personnel, captured consumer profiles, purchase histories, product needs, future purchasing plans and their feedback to target its marketing and product development better. As a result, Dell saw its market share rise from 1 per cent in 1990 to 9 per cent in 1997.

After implementing CRM, Telenor Mobil in Norway reduced their customer churn by 11 per cent and increased revenue from new mobile users by 50 per cent; the Royal Bank of Scotland reduced its marketing costs by reducing wastage, and increased its response rates (Reed, 1999).

According to Britt (1998), the underlying premise of CRM is that share of loyal customer spend, rather than share of market, maximises profitability. Developing tailored solutions for the most loyal and profitable customer is the 'solution killer strategy'.

According to *Credit Card Management* (1998), the banks would agree:

> Call it enterprise customer management ... Banks will be looking at their customer across all the functions of the bank ... The focal point has shifted from market share to share of customer spend.

2.5 RETURN ON INVESTMENT ON CRM SYSTEMS

Writing in 1993, Battles, Mark and Ryan point out that IT spending per white collar worker had tripled since 1980 and was projected to grow a further 60 per cent by 1999, accounting for 9.9 per cent of revenue. Investment in IT now represents 70 per cent of all capital investment. However, the return on this vast expenditure is by no means clear (Kelly, 1997).

For instance, the returns on data warehouses apparently are not well documented and, where measured, they often turn out to be poor. OTR group surveyed 1500 companies in six European Union countries and found that only 27 per cent of those who had implemented a data warehouse were able to identify a quantifiable financial benefit; 40 per cent did not even know the costs they had incurred. However, most expected to obtain non-financial benefits from their data warehouse – about 80 per

Only 27 per cent of those who had implemented a data warehouse were able to identify a quantifiable financial benefit.

cent of respondents were only able to identify non-financial benefits, but most thought that these benefits would be substantial. OTR also found that although the increase in revenue resulting from a data warehouse was approximately in line with expectations, cost reductions were significantly lower than expected and time taken to implement data warehousing was considerably longer than anticipated. Sixty per cent of respondents expected to implement their data warehouse within six months but only a quarter succeeded in doing so. OTR comments that there seem to be three main problems associated with this apparently poor performance: company data is not properly understood, leading to cost underestimates; pilot systems 'transform themselves' into production systems so companies lose track of costs; and complex, bespoke and/or combination software causes more difficulties than anticipated (OTR, 1997).

McKean (1999) found a more positive payback; firms surveyed were using a variety of methods, including Return on Investment, Return on Assets, Return on Equity, and traditional payback calculations, with hurdle rates ranging from 10 per cent to 25 per cent. Reported project size ranged from $1 million to $50 million, and payback periods were between six months and three years.

Some organisations prefer to generate an immediate return on their investment by using data marts – smaller data warehouses targeted to a single line of business or department. For example, Treasury Strategies Inc. surveyed 55 top banks and found that 34 (62 per cent) were mining data specifically to support cash management services (Gervino, 1998).

2.6 APPROACHES TO MEASURING RETURNS ON CRM INVESTMENTS

Wagle (1998) distinguishes between 'hard' returns, such as headcount, and 'soft' returns such as revenue or employee productivity gains. Based on his experiences of ERP, he argues that these investments are often made on faith, rather than good judgement. The payback is the Net Present Value (NPV) of the cost cuts attributable to the investment, minus any cost cuts that would have occurred in any case. Assuming the NPV is positive, the next step is to carry out a sensitivity analysis based on cost overruns, reductions in benefits, and time overruns.

The Sistrum report (Sistrum, 1998) considers economic and non-economic types of benefit from sales and marketing systems. The report makes the point that there are many 'soft' or hidden costs associated with the use of technology, such as training IT or data processing staff and sales and marketing staff, which have to be taken into account when assessing the return on marketing software investment. Maglitta (1997) suggests three measures of return, which he contrasts with return on investment (ROI). These are Business Value Added, Intangible Value, and Net Present Value.

Business Value Added of CRM systems is measured by the support they give to achieving business or marketing goals. An example would be: 'What was Information System's role in helping boost sales 10 per cent?' (Maglitta, 1997). Therefore, these may not be quantitative measures.

Effective CRM, in both consumer and business markets, increases value for the customer as well as the company.

Intangible Value is an evaluation of 'soft' benefits such as enhancing company reputation and attracting new staff, although Maglitta warns that quantitative benefits will probably have to be considered alongside the identification of this intangible value.

Net Present Value is Maglitta's preferred quantitative measure since it takes into account future benefits from the CRM investment, although he cautions against excessive concern about accuracy. The NPV figure, he says, should be considered as a ballpark figure, since forecasting is always tricky.

Pitt *et al.* (1995) have suggested a slightly different way of measuring IS service quality which focuses on the performance of the IS group as well as the systems, and which might be useful for internal monitoring of CRM systems performance. They suggest that the correct way of evaluating performance is based on system quality, information quality, use, user satisfaction, individual impact, organisational impact, and quality of the service and support provided by the IS department.

2.7 HOW MANAGERS WRITE THE BUSINESS CASE TODAY

There are a number of business drivers pushing CRM to the top of the corporate agenda. Most of the literature quoted in this report suggests that effective CRM, in both consumer and business markets, increases value for the customer as well as the company.

While this duality of benefit is intuitively obvious, one observes that most organisations focus upon the company benefit more than the benefit to customers. By not respecting the duality of benefit, it could mean that CRM investments do not pay back as expected because there is not enough value in the new business model to interest the customer.

This can be observed in many of the discussions centred on the business case for CRM. The early adopters of ambitious CRM projects that fit the definition described in Chapter 1, tended to start with 'acts of faith'. For instance, many Internet companies have still to turn a profit, yet they are highly prized for the quality of their relationships with customers. As CRM becomes more established, obvious strategies will emerge and early adopter experience will become more public. The next wave of adopters will probably not accept such a large change programme on faith alone. Managers in such companies are being asked to present and defend rigorous business cases for their proposed CRM programmes.

At the core of most business cases, there appears an estimate of the lifetime value of customer. At its crudest, this is a straight extrapolation from the past to arrive at differential values for customers and prospects. More sophisticated analysts look at the potential to enhance the profitability of certain customers through cross-selling, reference, reduced discounting and learning. Usually there is an exploration of how certain types of cost can be reduced through loyalty; these may include customer acquisition, marketing and service provision.

However, all but the straight-line extrapolation of the past depends on very subjective assessments and predications. There are few organisations with sufficient experience in a customer-centric environment to attach the same level of confidence to these new measures as they do to traditional discounted cash flows on a product portfolio. One other problem frequently encountered is that organisations do not necessarily have the data upon which to base complex calculations, such as differential cost to serve or true customer profitability. This can make a strategic review of the business case somewhat fraught and, at its worse, limits the imagination of management to that which is 'hard' and easily measured. Too often, costs are easier to measure than potential benefits, and partial solutions, called 'point solutions' by the IT industry, have benefits that are easier to quantify.

Most organisations turn to their marketers for leadership on customer strategy issues. However, the shift from product-based to customer-centric business models has challenged marketing's leadership role. One finds in most organisations that responsibility for customer management has diffused within the organisation and is often shared between marketing, sales and customer service.

One impact of this shared responsibility can be a lack of agreed measures of performance; a scorecard that tells the company how well it is serving its customers. In the days of product marketing, share of market, turnover and product margins were widely agreed goals and measures of success.

Shared responsibility for customers can mean differing and sometimes inconclusive measures. For example, many customer service functions look at the efficiency with which they process customer contacts and/or they measure customer satisfaction. Experienced CRM managers know that even satisfied customers sometimes defect; therefore satisfaction does not necessarily measure loyalty. The factors that keep the customer coming back for more, most often, are not the same that drive them away. Certainly, measures of operational performance such as call centre operator throughput, do not inform the company as to the customer value created at each contact.

Experienced CRM managers know that even satisfied customers sometimes defect; therefore satisfaction does not necessarily measure loyalty.

Tactically, marketing executives may focus on short-term measures of individual customer campaigns such as cross-selling, campaign response or cost per customer contact. These do not fully measure the strength of the customer relationship and its likelihood of creating shareholder value in the future. It is not proven that customers wish to be cross-sold to or that the best customers are necessarily promotion-sensitive. In fact, many would suggest that promotional campaigns attract inherently unprofitable customers. Cost measures, while important, miss the point that CRM investments are strategic and require appropriate measures for cost/benefit analysis.

Sales measures tend to be focused within discrete financial planning times and not necessarily aligned to lifetime values. In practice, one observes that sales executives are often divided into those who attract new customers and those who manage the existing customer base: the 'hunters' versus the 'farmers'. Sophisticated sales forces need different people who are rewarded differently for the two roles in recognition of the different processes and timescales for each.

2.8 CRM MEASUREMENT AND THE ROLE OF MARKETING

When it comes down to it, it is probably those in marketing who will need to find the right measures for CRM. It appears that these measures will go beyond market share. It also appears that more work needs to be done before a consensus emerges around measures of CRM achievement, but it is already generally accepted that these will focus on customer segments or, more likely, on individual customers.

Implicit in the desire to move towards individual customer relationships is the assumption that customers have different needs that can be addressed differently by the organisation. So, a good starting place in building the business case for CRM is a profound understanding of *differences* between customers with respect to behaviour, motivation, cost and their involvement with your organisation. Factors to consider against each are listed below.

Customer behaviour:

*   purchasing patterns – regularity, quantity, mix
*   emotional loyalty
*   purchasing process
*   referring other customers
*   providing feedback upon products and services
*   response to price and promotion.

Customer motivation:

*   the extent to which category choice is a conscious and involved decision versus an established habit
*   the extent to which the purchase is for functional versus emotional benefit
*   the desire for convenience, total solution, total experience
*   risk adversity
*   desire for advice and reassurance.

Cost of the customer:

- acquisition
- retention
- ongoing service
- defection.

Customer involvement:

- the extent to which the company has the credibility commensurate with its desired level of relationship
- frequency of customer contact
- breadth of customer contact
- importance of the company to the customer's total need
- quality of competitors.

Whether the CRM business case is developed by marketing, sales or customer service, the following questionnaire should help to determine your company's approach to CRM investment.

2.9 EXERCISE: ASSESS YOUR CRM BUSINESS CASE

Against each question, tick one box on the right according to how strongly you agree or disagree.

	disagree strongly	disagree	neither agree nor disagree	agree	agree strongly
1. My organisation has a well-grounded view as to how its CRM programme will create perceived value for our customers. Creating value for customers is as important to us as our own short-term profitability.	☐	☐	☐	☐	☐
2. As an organisation, we do not blindly follow rigid investment criteria and measures of shareholder value. We balance rigorous financial analysis with an intuitive understanding of our business and customers in determining investments.	☐	☐	☐	☐	☐
3. Our expectation of CRM is that we will learn from our customers about their different needs, behaviours and motivations.	☐	☐	☐	☐	☐
4. Our management information allows us to understand customer profitability.	☐	☐	☐	☐	☐
5. We approach CRM with a holistic view rather than build our CRM capability through a series of incremental solutions.	☐	☐	☐	☐	☐
6. Customer development is a well-organised business process within the organisation, which integrates marketing, sales and customer service functions.	☐	☐	☐	☐	☐
7. Our customer effort is monitored through a broad series of measures that reflect our success at adding value for customers as well as our ability to improve operational and sales effectiveness.	☐	☐	☐	☐	☐
Now score each tick as shown:	1	2	3	4	5
Enter your score per column in each box	☐	☐	☐	☐	☐

Total score:

How does your organisation score?

Score 7–14

Your organisation's CRM appears guided more by the value it wishes to extract from customers than the value it provides to them. The CRM programme may comprise no more than a series of individual projects that can be cost-justified, such as data mining, campaign management and call centres.

A careful series of initiatives should maintain a reasonable level of customer satisfaction and avoid the situation where your approach becomes dated. However, it is not equally certain that you will reap the full benefits of a loyal customer franchise and you may be at risk of losing key customers to more customer-focused organisations targeting your best ones.

Score 15–25

It is possible that your organisation's customer programme is inhibited by a number of management factors such as:

- overly rigid adherence to financial management policies

- a tendency to reduce vision into a series of pragmatic initiatives at the risk of not achieving the holistic vision

- lack of information that enables management to have a clear view of customers

- a lack of organisational learning and the ability to translate learning into action.

CRM touches on so many aspects of the organisation that it may be difficult to achieve without addressing some of the fundamental issues around defining and delivering the management vision.

Score 26–35

Your organisation has a vision around CRM that balances commercial opportunity with customer need. Managers want to learn from customers with a view to effecting change around customer needs. Management has the information needed to understand customers and match investment with opportunity. The organisation looks at CRM from a broad, holistic view and balances the need for financial prudence with commitment and insight.

2.10 EXERCISE: MARKETING AND CRM MEASUREMENT

Should marketing be tasked with building CRM measurements around customer behaviours, motivations, involvement and costs, the following diagnostic questionnaire may be useful:

Against each question, tick one box on the right according to how strongly you agree or disagree.

	disagree strongly	disagree	neither agree nor disagree	agree	agree strongly
1. Our customers exhibit dramatically different buying behaviours.	☐	☐	☐	☐	☐
2. Different customers have different motivations.	☐	☐	☐	☐	☐
3. Each of our customers has different costs associated with their recruitment, development and maintenance.	☐	☐	☐	☐	☐
4. Our corporate (product) brand is highly credible with customers and can sustain the type of customer relationships that we wish to enter. We are actively engaged with customers and represent an important part of their needs in the market place.	☐	☐	☐	☐	☐
Now score each tick as shown:	1	2	3	4	5
Enter your score per column in each box	☐	☐	☐	☐	☐

Total score:

How does your organisation score?

Score 4–8

There is either very little differentiation across your customer base or you lack the necessary information to identify the differences.

In markets where customers have very similar needs and costs to serve, one must be careful not to create differences that add little customer value. This will tend to add cost to your business for which customers will not pay and which will stretch the credibility of your company's reputation. Not all businesses can legitimately sustain relationship marketing.

On the other hand, if your score reflects a lack of sufficient understanding of customer behaviour, motivation, cost or attachment to your organisation, you may be at risk to competitors that do have that understanding. Clever new entrants will target the most profitable customers, leaving the incumbents with the less profitable ones.

Score 9-14

There are clearly some differences between customers, and the marketing challenge is to focus upon the drivers that differentiate the most with a view to creating unique and relevant measures to support differing value propositions.

Score 15-20

Your customer base is highly differentiated along most factors so the marketing challenge is to find the right intersections of differentiators in order to create a manageable number of measures and value propositions. There may be clear links between different customer behaviours and motivations; this will simplify the funnelling process. Implementing CRM is likely to pay off in recognisable ways for your organisation.

In markets where customers have very similar needs and costs to serve, one must be careful not to create differences that add little customer value.

In the next chapter, we consider how CRM can be implemented on a step by step basis involving customers, front-office staff and technology, and the customisation of relationships and the offer.

3

Implementing CRM

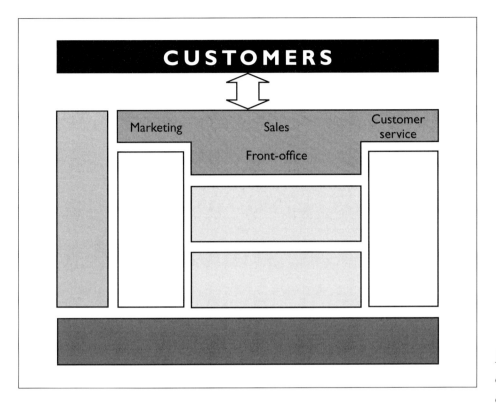

Retaining existing customers is far less costly than trying to attract new ones.

Organisations that can apply the right strategic mix of technology, structures, people and processes will create a strong customer relationship environment which focuses on the right customers (Galbreath, 1998).

As has already been discussed, customer loyalty is becoming increasingly important for organisations as they realise that retaining existing customers is far less costly than trying to attract new ones (Morris, 1994). This is particularly true for supermarket and high-street shops in the UK, with the introduction of 'loyalty' cards that reward customers with bonuses and discounts. Morris discusses the costs of losing customers, which can be far greater than the value of sales foregone because of negative word of mouth. He cites Ohio State University Hospital, which developed a Patient Satisfaction Measurement System in 1991. Forty-five dissatisfied patients refused to return, costing the hospital $164 200 (or $815 000 over five years); the hospital estimated the revenue lost from other patients as a result of negative word of mouth as an *additional* $600 000 over five years (Morris, 1994).

3.1 TEN RECOMMENDATIONS FOR IMPLEMENTING CRM

Computer Sciences Corporation (1999b) reported on a study tour exploring future trends in customer relationship management and drew up ten recommendations for the implementation of CRM:

1   There is a need for a strategic approach to customer relationship management.

> Survey your customers to determine which mix of customer communications channels would be best for the business. Examine the characteristic behaviour of the 80 per cent of your customers most important to you to ensure the convenience of the selected channels. Only then invest in best-of-breed technology to support these channels.

Develop formal processes to enable the contact centre to provide feedback on customer issues to the entire company.

2   The integration of multiple call centres will deliver business value.

> Integrate all of the organisation's call centres into a single virtual call centre with focused management and the ability to balance workload and provide backup.

3   Customer relations will benefit from extending the role of the call centre.

> Create a single point of contact for customers across the chosen channels by extending the responsibility of the call centre organisation to handle all communications with customers other than those handled by the face-to-face sales and service groups. This contact centre will also be a single point of contact within the enterprise for customer relationship matters.

4   The flow of information from the contact centre can be used to improve business processes.

> Develop formal processes to enable the contact centre to provide feedback on customer issues to the entire company. Ensure that affected departments and workgroups have corresponding processes to utilise this valuable customer information.

5   Build the ability to handle business through whatever media the customer chooses.

> Equip the contact centre with the technology necessary to integrate the handling of mail, e-mail, fax and Web communications with the handling of telephone calls.

6   As the role of the contact centre extends, you must raise the quality of the staff and their management.

> Staff the contact centre with highly qualified, trained personnel. Pay them well, equip them fully, and pay special attention to motivating and managing them well.

7   The change from support only to support and sales must be business-driven.

> Ensure that the contact centre's measurements and compensation practices are aligned with the organisation's overall marketing strategy.

8   Interactive Voice Response (IVR) can turn your customers on or off.

> Review your organisation's IVR scripts to ensure that they are of high quality and in keeping with the approved corporate image – and that they reflect your customers' needs and ways of approaching your products and services.

9   Continuous-speech-recognition IVRs can transform the effectiveness of customer processes.

> Look at opportunities presented by continuous-speech-recognition IVRs to reduce the cost of current customer-service applications and, more importantly, to enable entirely new approaches to the customer relationship.

10 The technology now provides an opportunity to take a global view of customer interaction.

> Never underestimate the value of any interaction with the customer, however it happens. What one customer says, many customers may be thinking – and it may be the only time you hear the feedback.

Never underestimate the value of any interaction with the customer, however it happens.

3.2 STEP BY STEP CRM IMPLEMENTATION

Peppers, Rogers and Dorf (1999) suggest that there are four key steps for putting a one-to-one marketing programme to work: identifying customers; differentiating among them; interacting with them; and customising the products or services to fit each individual customer's needs. These steps are outlined in Fig. 3.1.

FIGURE 3.1

The four steps to implementing CRM

---

1 Identifying customers

Activity	*Steps to consider*
Collect and enter more customer names into the existing database	• Use an outside service for scanning or data entry
Collect additional information about your customers	• Swap names with a noncompetitive company in your field
Verify and update customer data and delete outdated information	• Use drip-irrigation dialogue – ask your customers one or two questions every time you are in touch with them
	• Put your customer files through a 'spring cleaning'
	• Run your database through the National Change of Address (NCOA) file

2 Differentiating among customers

Activity	*Steps to consider*
Identify your organisation's top customers	• Using last year's sales or other simple, readily available data, take your best guess at identifying the top 5 per cent of your customers

Determine which customers cost your organisation money	• Look for simple rules to isolate the bottom 20 per cent of your customers (such as customers who haven't ordered in more than a year or those who always bid you out) and reduce the amount of mail you send them
Select several companies you really want to do business with next year	• Add them to your database and record at least three contact names per company
Find higher-value customers who have complained about your product or service more than once in the last year	• Baby-sit their orders, put a product or quality-assurance person in touch with them ASAP to check on your progress
Look for last year's large customers who have ordered half as much or less this year	• Go visit them now, before your competition does
Find customers who buy only one or two products from your company but a lot from other businesses	• Make them an offer they can't refuse to try several more items from you
Rank customers into A, B, and C categories, roughly based on their value to your company (Don't try to isolate the top 5 per cent or bottom 20 per cent – any 'blunt instrument' criterion such as annual spending or years doing business with the company will work)	• Decrease marketing activities and spending for the Cs and use the savings to fund increased activities for the As

Call your competitors to compare their customer service with yours.

3 Interact

Activity

If you are focusing on channel members, call the top three people at your top 5 per cent of customers

Call your own company and ask questions, see how hard it is to get through and get answers

Call your competitors to compare their customer service with yours

Use incoming calls as selling opportunities

Evaluate the voice response unit at your customer information centre

Steps to consider

• Don't try to sell – just talk and make sure they are happy

• Test eight to ten different scenarios as a 'mystery shopper'. Record the calls and critique them

• Repeat the above activity

• Offer specials, closeouts, and trial offers

• Make the recordings sound friendlier, be more helpful, and move customers through the system faster

through your organisation to customers

Initiate more dialogue with valuable customers

	cycle times to speed up your response times
	• Print personalised messages on invoices, statements, and envelopes
	• Have sales reps sign personal letters rather than mass-mailing letters signed by a senior manager
	• Have the right people in your organisation call the right customer executives. (That is, have your CIO call another CIO, or have the VP of marketing call the business owner)
	• Call every valuable customer your company has lost in the last two years and give them a reason to return

Use technology to make doing business with your company easier

	• Gather the e-mail addresses of your customers in order to follow up with them
	• Offer alternative means of communication
	• Consider using fax back and fax broadcast systems
	• Scan customer information into the database

Improve complaint handling

	• Plot how many complaints you receive each day and work to improve the ratio of complaints handled on the first call

4 Customize

Activity

Customise paperwork to save your customers time and your company money

Personalise your direct mail

Fill out forms for your customers

Steps to consider

• Use regional and subject-specific versions of catalogues

• Use customer information to individualise offers

• Keep the mailings simple

• Use laser equipment to save time and make you look smarter

they want to hear from you	personal visits as the customer specifies
Find out what your customers want	• Invite customers to focus groups or discussion meetings to solicit their reactions to your products, policies and procedures
Ask your top ten customers what you can do differently to improve your product or service	• Respond to their suggestions
	• Follow up and repeat the process
Involve top management in customer relations	• Give them lists of questions to ask based on the history of individual customers

(*Source:* Peppers, Rogers and Dorf, 1999)

3.3 LINKING BACK-OFFICE AND FRONT-OFFICE SYSTEMS

Technology plays an important part in tracking customer information and measuring return on investment for individual companies. In order to successfully implement CRM an organisation needs to understand about back-office and front-office systems. The US West Case below illustrates this point.

In order to successfully implement CRM an organisation needs to understand about back-office and front-office systems.

Case study • US WEST

US West exploits technology to implement its revolutionary Customer Relationship Management Strategy

Created in 1984, US West has 97 per cent of the market for local telephone services within its territory, but it knows the monopoly days are numbered. US West management watched the steady erosion of AT&T's share of the long-distance market when its monopoly ended, and became determined to avoid the same fate. To determine how to compete successfully in a deregulated future, it conducted an exhaustive strategic review of its business. The result is the Customer Relationship Management Strategy (CRMS), a $100 million revamp that will move the company away from its old focus on telephone numbers and build a new company-wide culture that centres on the customer.

The study resulted in the determination that US West must convert the majority of its 25 million customers from telephone users paying $20 a month (the average bill) to service clients paying $400 a month. It plans to achieve this by offering customers a range of new products and services that meet their needs. It is aggressively exploiting telecommunications technology to create new offerings such as Caller ID, Voice Messaging, Call Waiting and ADSL (Asynchronous Digital Subscriber Loop) for very high-speed Internet access from the home or office. It is also moving to solutions that are hard to compete with. It believes it can achieve differentiation through integration.

By providing services which package voice and data, wireless and wireline, local and long distance through a single bill and a single contact point in case of difficulties, it believes that it can 'make life better and easier for millions of customers'. It believes that its integrated service will make it difficult for competitors to pick off services one at a time, thus leading to growth in revenue and profits for US West.

Innovative products are not enough

The CRMS study indicated that product packaging would be insufficient to build the necessary customer loyalty unless it was accompanied by superb customer service. If it can build a relationship that its customers perceive to be worth retaining even when competitors offer specific services at more competitive prices, US West expects to be able to defend and even extend its market presence. To do this, it must put in place systems that enable employees, whether a call-centre agent or a service technician calling at the door, to treat customers personally. US West recognises that the same infrastructure that makes an employee aware of the customer's recent complaint can also be used to turn the 3 500 technicians who install equipment into salesmen armed with detailed information about the customers and scripts to help them sell.

The company will also respond personally when customers experience a service failure. The CRMS system will ensure that they receive a call from a marketing representative empowered to provide various forms of compensation, such as two months' free phone service.

Identifying profitable customers is difficult but essential

One problem addressed by the CRMS programme is the recognition that not all customers are equally profitable; some will never be profitable. Telecommunications industry studies have shown that as much as 80 per cent of profits can come from as few as 3 per cent of the buildings in a company's territory. Determining which customers are profitable has not been easy for US West, particularly as it recognises that customer profitability is not static. It values the potential lifetime revenue from the customer, not just the current income stream.

Once this definition of profitability was adopted, the project team went on to find analysis tools that mine customer data to determine which customers match the characteristics of an unprofitable customer. The next step will be to subtly encourage such customers to leave the fold. The final challenge is to ensure that no US West marketing group spends money on programmes designed to lure that customer back!

(*Source:* Computer Sciences Corporation, 1998)

In Chapter 4, we consider the strategic approaches to building a CRM programme and the increasing need for connectivity between front-office and back-office systems with the Internet and e-business developments.

4

The components of CRM

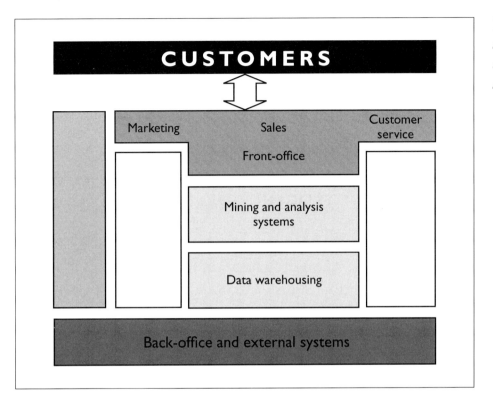

The 'heart' of CRM architecture is the data warehousing and analysis systems.

Many companies begin their CRM programmes from one of two places: data warehousing or customer service call centres.

The 'heart' of CRM architecture is the data warehousing and analysis systems. This permits one view of the customer, facilitates a segmentation of the customer base, and provides some immediate business benefit in terms of marketing campaigns.

However, call centres are a priority for many companies struggling to cope with the demands of customers for more immediate service at any hour of the day. The next step is usually to expand the programme into contact points other than the call centre (sales force, stores, web sites) and to integrate business intelligence with the emerging front-office.

From there, implementation moves into its most difficult stage, the integration of the front-office with the company's back-office or fulfilment systems. Issues of culture, control and information systems often arise. Many start-ups have built their systems for the modern, online and interactive customer economy, so for them there is little problem. However, most large organisations today have a variety of back-office systems and processes that have been painstakingly developed over the past twenty years or so. High levels of integration can be problematic. For some, the back-office systems are so complex, expensive and inflexible, that full integration of the front-office must wait for a large-scale back-office change programme and the implementation of new technology. There is a natural tension between those who wish to 'manage from the future' using new interactive technologies, and those who wish 'to fix that which is broken' in the fulfilment systems first before allowing customers to determine their own offers. There is no easy answer to this dilemma!

4.1 BUSINESS INTELLIGENCE AND DATA WAREHOUSING

The market for business intelligence software has grown rapidly in recent years and in 1997 was worth somewhere between US$6.3 billion and US$8.5 billion. The Palo Alto Management Group has identified more than two hundred large companies offering database aggregation systems (Rosen, 1998).

For an organisation to maximise the potential benefits of its information requires a change of attitude so that data is treated and managed as an asset (Levitin and Redman, 1998; Wang *et al.*, 1998; Cesare and Salaun, 1995). In the majority of cases, this also implies substantial investment in technologies that store and manage data. However, it is widely suggested that it is not simply possession of the technology that confers a competitive advantage on organisations but a balanced approach involving advanced technology, a focus on customer-related processes such as order fulfilment or CRM, and a concentration on customer needs (Brown, 1996; Simmons, 1996). In order to achieve this, information systems have to be integrated with marketing. This requires some degree of functional, as well as technical integration (Jiang *et al.*, 1997; Saaksjarvi and Talvinen, 1993; Shaw and Stone, 1988). Polaroid is a case in point.

Case study ● POLAROID

In 1995 Polaroid linked its performance review process to CRM. Polaroid is reaching out to its customers more and emphasises the personal dialogue. The sales rep develops a relationship with the customer out in the field and does not just complete a sales transaction. Such a process is strategic in nature as the sales rep targets customers that should be visited. A technological platform has been set up that allows information to be collected about customers, inputted and shared throughout the organisation.

Banks have traditionally used their customer information databases to support product marketing, although not always on an enterprise-wide basis. This has sometimes resulted in customers being bombarded with inappropriate and unsuitable offers. However, recent increases in bad debt and the competitive inroads of new suppliers (Broady-Preston and Hayward, 1998) have encouraged the banks to take a customer-centred approach (Rosenthal and McEachern, 1997). Integrated systems can make major improvements to bank marketing. Conversely, failure to develop integrated marketing information can leave some banks at a great disadvantage (Gerson, 1998). There has also been a shift of emphasis; risk is now not just about potential losses that a bank or credit agency might sustain, but about profit opportunities it might miss (*Credit Card Management*, 1998; Fuglseth and Gronhaug, 1994). Therefore, the interest in a good data stream and information systems in banking is growing (Ravichandran and Banerjee, 1994).

4.2 DIRECT MARKETING AND DATABASE MARKETING (DBM)

One-to-one marketing is only possible with the help of customer databases and front-office systems, such as interactive media (Pitta, 1998; Pearce, 1997; Stern and Barton, 1997; Gronroos, 1996). Just having information about customers, however, will not in itself deliver competitive advantage; there needs to be a change of business philosophy from the push approach of traditional 4Ps marketing to a relationship marketing perspective of collaboration with customers and two-way communication (Gronroos, 1996).

Just having information about customers, however, will not in itself deliver competitive advantage; there needs to be a change of business philosophy.

Unfortunately, all too often direct marketing has implied mass marketing; product focused and impersonal. However, even comparatively simple profiling techniques can increase response rates and profits. Various authors describe the incorporation of recency, frequency and monetary value (RFM) information into a customer database to determine the customers most likely to respond to marketing initiatives. Simple profit, however, is no guarantee that the company will increase shareholder value through its database marketing. Database marketing should target those customers whose return exceeds the investment needed to acquire and retain them (Hansotia, 1996).

Customer databases used as part of a relationship marketing strategy can have powerful results. One North American bank trebled the number of products sold per household in two years using customer profiling; database marketing has also reduced mailing sizes for direct campaigns by up to two-thirds (Adolf *et al.*, 1997). At Federal Express, a campaign targeted at small businesses did 130 per cent better and brought in 65 per cent more revenue than a similar mass marketing effort (Foley, 1997).

So what prevents organisations from adopting database marketing, if the potential benefits are so great? One study looked at barriers to the successful implementation of database marketing across several industries and found that cost overall is seen as the biggest barrier. In the retail and travel industries where they are more likely to achieve a competitive advantage from their IT investment, management consider organisational and strategic barriers as more significant while financial services perceive technical barriers as the main problem (Desai *et al.*, 1998). In the UK, the strategic barriers to the implementation of database marketing in financial services organisations include the lack of a DBM strategy, poor marketing orientation and insufficient board level backing (Fletcher and Wright, 1995). Other studies have found that failure to understand the potential of DBM is a significant inhibitor, which may possibly be connected to problems of design or ownership (Lewington *et al.*, 1996).

As Belfer (1998) says, 'IT are from Mars, and Marketing are from Venus'. This sentiment is supported by a later study by Fletcher and Wright (1997) who found that adoption of database marketing systems is linked with the strategic importance given to direct marketing, as well as strategic integration of IT and marketing, and the provision of significant marketing resources.

Finally, many advocates of relationship marketing stress the importance of two-way communication between supplier and customer, of the need to listen as well as to sell (Haynes *et al.*, 1992).

4.3 DATA WAREHOUSES

> Banks tend to be rich in data but poor in information.
> (VP, Great Western Bank, quoted in Orenstein 1997)

Kelly (1996) argues that there are only three ways in which an organisation can increase its revenue: acquiring new customers; cross-selling; or extending the duration of the customer relationship. He believes that cross-selling and customer retention are only now appearing on the marketing agenda because of the capabilities offered by data warehousing.

Existing databases or other IT systems are not always easy to use for relationship marketing purposes, although some organisations have managed to do so (McKendrick, 1995). Online transactions processing (OLTP) systems may lack integration, with data fragmented across multiple sources. The data will also be formatted for transactions processing so it is inefficiently organised for queries. OLTP systems have to be good at reading and writing tiny amounts of data within a predictable part of the database; data warehouses have to read huge amounts of data from across the entire data warehouse, with no prior notice. Querying an online, transactions processing database may be difficult; it may require programming expertise and such queries may reduce the speed at which transactions are processed (Kelly, 1997). For this reason, data warehouses are usually constructed and operated offline and are built to act as decision support. Important features of a data warehouse are scalability, extensibility and flexibility (Kelly, 1997), as well as its capability to provide statistical and optimisation modelling through a flexible, user-friendly interface (Sisodia, 1992). Ten critical success factors of data warehouse projects are identified by Kelly (op cit., p. 68):

1. information
2. ease of access
3. data standards
4. dedicated resource
5. adequate performance
6. corporate sponsorship
7. operationally stable
8. agreed infrastructure
9. new user culture
10. source data.

Kelly and Boon (1996) list seventeen causes of failure in data warehouse projects. These include inability to cost-justify the data warehouse, the IT department acting both as the principal drivers of a data warehouse project while assuming the protection function, and too few users having the skills needed to exploit the data warehouse properly.

Investments in data warehouses are considerable. Global spending on data warehouses in financial services was expected to rise from US$2.1 billion in 1995 to US$5.4 billion in 1999 (Orenstein, 1997). Although hardware costs are falling, software costs may actually be increasing, particularly as one supplier projects that banks will increasingly see the need for two data warehouses; one for querying and modelling, the other for sales and marketing (Orenstein, 1997).

NCR is one of the companies that have focused on scalable data warehouses and high-availability transaction processing, via its NCR Teradata system which is targeting the financial services industry. The company is aiming to develop ATMs as customer service points where bank customers will be able to connect over the Internet to theatres and airlines, and even buy tickets that will then be printed out by the ATM (Groenfeldt, 1997). Other frequently mentioned vendors of data warehouses are Oracle and Sybase. Sweat and Riggs (1999) outline the recent products of the predominant vendors of software related to CRM.

Some vendors have packaged their data warehouse with data mining and vertical applications to enable better understanding of customers and provide more effective decision support systems. Key players here are Informix, SAS Institute and IBM. Informix has a decision support system called Decision Frontier that combines data mining and vertical applications for telecoms, retail, finance and manufacturing industries. SAS has Warehouse Administrator and Enterprise Miner, and it has an agreement with Exchange Applications Inc. to include links to its Valex marketing automation software (Neil, 1998; Stedman, 1997). SAS was one of the largest data warehousing companies in 1997 with revenues of US$750 million. In the same year, SAS invested 32 per cent of its revenues – US$240 million – in software development, and it achieves consistent annual customer retention of 98 per cent.

IBM has DB2, a repository that stores images and allows operators to identify image texture, colour, ink and other factors. Perhaps the most famous customer of DB2 is the Vatican, which is using it to store images of priceless ancient manuscripts (Halper, 1996).

4.4 DATA MINING

Data mining is the process of digging into an organisation's data warehouse to identify patterns and trends. Often, complex data mining tools are used to uncover previously unknown links or patterns. Data mining is defined as using software to identify patterns in data that would not otherwise be apparent.

The business intelligence data mining provides is driving CRM programmes and competitive strategy (Kilbane, 1998). It is claimed that more than four-fifths of Fortune 500 companies believe data mining will have been a critical factor for business success by the year 2000 (Baker and Baker, 1998). One organisation that has made data mining work to deliver its phenomenal business success is Capital One, the US financial services company. Using data mining to profile individual customers in great detail helped Capital One to become one of the top ten credit card issuers in the USA within three years.

Information systems are being used in two ways by executives: to address specific questions/problems, and to scan without a specific question in mind. The former use helps improve business efficiency, and the latter helps managers to challenge their existing assumptions about the business and develop creative new strategies (Vandenbosch and Huff, 1997).

Data mining is defined as using software to identify patterns in data that would not otherwise be apparent.

Four key data mining methodologies are: affinity analysis; clustering; predictive modelling; and segmentation.

Affinity analysis looks for patterns in customer behaviour that may not have been observed previously, such as the tendency of customers to buy orange juice and cold remedies at the same time.

Clustering puts customers into similar groups based on certain attributes or behaviours. The Chase Manhattan case below illustrates this.

Case study • **CHASE MANHATTAN**

Chase's vision is to create price lifestyle-focused packages for customers by using a single platform to support every product, segment, channel and market across the consumer bank. To achieve growth by getting closer to customers, Chase relies on direct customer experience aligned with data and information from historical, demographic and psychographic sources. This allows the bank to conduct a pattern analysis of the data, observing issues with some customers and projecting that into a larger database to find similar clusters.

Predictive modelling uses historical purchase data plus information about promotions to predict future behaviour. It is particularly useful in targeting mailshots or other promotional activity and improving the response rates, and hence payback, on marketing initiatives.

Segmentation is closely linked to clustering; it can help organisations to identify the type of customer they most want to attract and to keep and to develop tailored offers (McKim, 1998). Chase Manhattan, for example, mines data from various sources to develop attractive offers for its customers. For these reasons, data mining is most effective where organisations can link transactions to specific customers (Saarenvirta, 1998).

Data mining applications

As with data warehousing, the tendency for data mining is integration. The suppliers of data mining software are forming alliances with other software suppliers. In fact, it has been claimed that most analysts think there is no future for independent data mining houses. Oracle has an agreement with seven data mining suppliers to integrate their products with its Oracle 8.1 database. These are Angoss, DataMind, Datasage, Information Discovery, SPSS, SRA International and Thinking Machines (Foley and Russell, 1998). Thinking Machines also has a partnership with Paragren Technologies to integrate data mining with Paragren's analytical marketing applications in order to offer enterprise relationship marketing (PR Newswire, 1998). The benefits are expected to be a closer link between data mining and campaign management, offering the capability for customers to focus their marketing campaigns better.

One industry in which data mining has become an important adjunct to marketing strategy is retailing. Safeway, for example, has been using data from its loyalty cards since 1990 to analyse customer data down to product level using IBM's Intelligent Miner software. The company can then send out carefully targeted mailshots to its customers (Manchester, 1998). Wal-Mart is a famed user of data mining, identifying its most popular products day by day and changing the store layout to ensure that customers 'bump into' these products (Halper, 1996).

Other industries have been able to build up their databases with a view to data mining by consolidating the information gathered from field-based microprocessors (i.e. mobile- and embedded-computing). Federal Express, for example, has tens of thousands of processors in the field, ranging from the 'supertracker' package-tracking and scanning devices carried by its delivery personnel, to PCs in customers' mailrooms that were supplied by

Federal Express. While these processors were originally introduced to improve the efficiency of Federal Express's operations, the data is now stored in a data warehouse so that summaries can be forwarded to departmental data marts where they are analysed to understand customers better (Whiting and Caldwell, 1999).

The UK electricity companies are also using data mining to help them compete in Europe. Scottish Power is using a WhiteCross WX9010 system to evaluate customers, which was set up by ManWeb whom they acquired in 1995 (Couldwell, 1998).

Financial services companies are increasingly using data mining to understand why customers act in the way they do; the application of this knowledge to marketing is helping to increase customer profitability through better customer profiling and improved credit risk data (Fabris, 1998).

Big claims are made about the impact of data mining on profitability, although few are quantified.

Bank of America and Citibank have both used data mining for management and marketing applications – fraud prevention, credit scoring, cross-selling opportunities and marketing campaigns (Talmor, 1996). This capability allows banks to become active rather than passive in their relationships with customers:

> With new tools, for example, banks can now begin to act more like stores than relatively passive lending and depository institutions ... They can now aggressively market a panoply of products and services, with the conviction that the flow of capital is actually affected by the flow of information.
>
> (Makos, 1995).

A consequence will be that banks ask their data warehouses more demanding questions, so the ways in which they can segment and subsequently target those segments will become increasingly complex (Disney, 1995).

Big claims are made about the impact of data mining on profitability, although few are quantified. One vendor of data warehousing and data mining products, Red Brick, does claim that its data mining tools should add one percentage point to the operating margin of one of its customers, Longs Drug Stores (Kessler, 1997). Evans (1996) claims that customer management is particularly important in industries with huge disparities in customer profitability, such as banking where 50 per cent or more of customers may be unprofitable.

Customer concerns about data mining are primarily about privacy. A Harris study found that over three-quarters of respondents thought that businesses generally asked for too much information, and four out of five expressed concern about threats to personal privacy. Over 60 per cent said that this concern arose from the collection and use of custom-tailored information about their interests, purchases and viewing habits (Weisman, 1995).

One area that does *not* seem to be a concern for users of data mining tools is the purchase price. Despite prices ranging from US$1000 to more than US$100 000, only 5 per cent of companies not yet using data mining software cited price as the reason (Foley and Russell, 1998).

The shift in the last two to three years has been towards integration, visualisation and data access tools. Data mining, together with artificial intelligence, are the key technological areas cited in the 1997 Gartner Group survey as impacting most on business development (Baker and Baker, 1998). Future developments include highly sophisticated software that will be able to interpret text and analyse the structure of sentences and inflection (Vernon, 1998). More immediately, Charles Schwab is working on data mining incoming e-mails to separate urgent from non-urgent messages (Stedman, 1997).

4.5 IT AND MARKETING SYSTEMS

Sheth and Sisodia (1995) believe that IT could improve, and eventually alter, marketing practice in several ways, including lowering the cost of providing a particular service and reducing the demand for personnel-based customer service. They argue that for sustained competitive advantage, companies need an IT platform that uniquely blends core marketing competencies with seamless technology.

Mazur (1993) cites research by Price Waterhouse showing that over 70 per cent of respondents thought the importance of sales and marketing systems was increasing. Meredith (1996) found rather more equivocal results in IT; although 67 per cent of respondents were satisfied with their IT systems, over 80 per cent also said there was a gap between what IT should deliver and what it actually delivers. Meredith reports that some types of CRM software are more likely to deliver benefits than others (Fig. 4.1).

System	Benefits % users	System	Benefits % users
Post coding software	Most users	Call Centre/CTI	73%
Territory Mgt/GIS	Most users	Marketing Dbase software	59%
Word processing, spreadsheets	91% 91%	Internet	43%
Contact Mgt software	80%	Statistical analysis software	20%
Lead tracking	76%	Telemarketing	17%

(*Source:* adapted from Meredith, 1996)

FIGURE 4.1

CRM software systems and beneficiaries

4.6 FRONT-OFFICE AUTOMATION

There are a number of areas where technology plays a part in managing customer relationships. The call centre and the Internet with its emerging e-business applications are two areas where more effective relationships with customers can be achieved.

4.7 THE CALL CENTRE

Initially, call centres were associated with activities such as making travel reservations, checking bank accounts and ordering goods from catalogues. Recently, they have spread to other industries so that there were 70 000 formal call centres in the USA in 1998, with numbers increasing at 20 per cent per year (Computer Sciences Corporation, 1998). There are fewer call centres in Europe generally, but in the UK their numbers are increasing at about 45 per cent per year. Thus, call centres are becoming a major channel for dealing with customer communications.

Call centres have been a significant part of the CRM operations in banks and financial services firms for a number of years now. They seem to offer major opportunities for improvement, if properly managed. Reed (1997) claims that:

> According to CAP Gemini, 30 per cent of the £3 240 million being spent annually on call centre operations is wasted through inefficiency, poor equipment and poor staffing.

Having said that, there are instances of considerable profit improvement as a result of using call centre technology. Sometimes, changing just a few processes can have a considerable impact on profitability; Mosaic/Techguide investigated the possible savings by automating order fulfilment processes and found that one customer service centre, with 154 processes, secured estimated savings of US$102 363 per annum by automating just four of these processes. In another study of a call centre for credit and collections, potential savings of US$1.5 million per year were identified from automated fulfilment and call management, including screen pops. Half of these savings were in staff costs (techguide.com, 1998). Savings also result from an increased focus on target customers. Johnson *et al.* (1995) suggest that, with careful targeting of its offerings, a telephone-based bank can obtain a 30 to 40 per cent cost advantage over traditional banks.

In the computer industry, Compaq uses technology to integrate its customer information for service support.

Case study • COMPAQ

Compaq is an example of a company that uses technology to help track sales more effectively. Through the use of intranets and extranets, Compaq is integrating all of its call centres, its entire sales force around the world, some 30 000 resellers, and all of its existing and potential customers into the same database. So all information is located in an integrated system, which will enhance customer relationships.

Grant and Schlesinger (1995) report on an upgrading project in an airline reservation centre which led to the improvements shown in Fig. 4.2.

Costs	Improvement
Average call US$3	−35%
Total costs US$250m, of which labour 80%	
10% of calls result in a booking	+100%
Average revenue per call US$10	+50%

(*Source:* Grant and Schlesinger, 1995)

FIGURE 4.2

Performance improvements in an airline call centre

Overall, the result was a 400 per cent increase in profit contribution from this reservation centre.

A third example of savings through call centre technology comes from The Netherlands, where Informatie Beheer Group implemented and later outsourced its call centre which resulted in savings of 30 per cent on telephone costs between 1992 and 1995 (Thiadens *et al.*, 1995).

Anton et al. (1995) investigated the consequences of putting insufficient resources into a call centre. He tracked 6500 unanswered calls at a consumer electronics company, and found that 38 per cent of customers planned to return their goods to a store and exchange them for another brand.

Case study ● **US WEST INC.**

As a phone company, US West Inc. understands the need for good phone support so it is investing in its call centre operations in an effort to improve its service.

US West Inc. rolled out a custom-built call handling system in 1997. A central-office switch in Denver accepts calls from 14 states and routes them to the most available agent in one of 13 call centres nationwide. 'The system allows us to hit our target, which is 80 per cent of the time the phone gets answered in three rings,' says David Laube, US West Inc.'s VP and CIO.

In 1998, US West Inc. opened a $6 million centre in Pocatello, Idaho, and a $4 million centre in Helena, Montana; another will open in Idaho Falls, Idaho during 1999. The call centres are showing results. The Helena centre has improved its average speed of answering by 30 per cent, while call volume has more than doubled. The Pocatello centre, which makes outbound calls focused on customer satisfaction, reports that 95 per cent of the customers it contacts are satisfied with their phone service.

(*Source:* Sweat and Hibbard, 1999)

Although call centres have had a major impact on customer service capabilities, future trends are towards greater use of the Web. This is because of the economics: the average cost of a banking transaction is $1.08 when made in person at a bank branch, 54 cents when made through a call centre, and 13 cents in an Internet-based, self-care environment (Hoard, 1999).

4.8 E-BUSINESS APPLICATIONS AND CONNECTIVITY

60 000 people log onto the Internet for the first time every day in the USA; worldwide, the traffic over the Internet doubles every 100 days.

Technology is moving at a fast pace. Today, 60 000 people log onto the Internet for the first time every day in the USA; worldwide, the traffic over the Internet doubles every 100 days (Harari, 1999). The Internet and the World Wide Web are widely accessible to most organisations around the world. The number of host computers was projected to grow to more than 100 million by the end of the 1990s, with an estimated 1 million plus commercial web sites during 2000 (de Kare-Silver, 1997). In an ever-shrinking global environment, customers can access products/services over the Web, 24 hours a day throughout the whole year. Total commerce over the Net is forecast to reach $200 billion by 2000, of which $17 billion will be business to consumer (de Kare-Silver, 1998). Two examples of business to consumer transactions taking place over the Web are new car purchases and online share dealing. While only 2 per cent of non-fleet new car sales in the USA were referrals from web sites in 1997, it is predicted that by the end of 2000 one-third of all new car purchasers will have used the Web (Hagel and Singer, 1999). Charles Schwab doubled its web-based trading accounts to $1.8 million (worth $2 billion of securities per week) in one year, which accounts for over 50 per cent of trading volume (Computer Sciences Corporation, 1998). The arrival of digital television will increase customers' ability to buy electronically from suppliers anywhere in the world, leading to price levelling. Moreover, the Internet will create more opportunities for strategic alliances between businesses (MCA, 1999). To manage such a customer environment is challenging at best and it has been suggested that ownership of customer information and management of the customer relationship will become the province of 'infomediaries' (Hagel and Singer, 1999).

'Infomediary' is a term used increasingly in e-business circles. It describes an expected phenomenon whereby a few web-based companies will become major intermediaries of commerce done over the Internet due to the consumer and supplier information that they hold. Informed Internet commentators predict that it will be in the consumer's interest to concentrate their online purchases across a few trusted companies who have a comprehensive understanding of their needs, motivations, preferences and budgets. These consumer agents will be trusted to maintain privacy and security of transactions and to vet the suppliers they offer to consumers. Suppliers of goods and services who do not enjoy such a relationship with consumers will find it more profitable to work with the infomediaries than to try to replicate their consumer relationships.

It seems increasingly likely that e-commerce will be driven by agents acting for buyers and sellers as the market matures.

It seems increasingly likely that e-commerce will be driven by agents acting for buyers and sellers as the market matures. Consumers will wish to guard themselves from poor marketing, cross-selling, people selling profile information about them to third parties, insecure transactions and so on. Moreover, consumers will soon realise the value of the information about themselves that they currently provide to sellers for free, and they may even demand to be rewarded in some way for releasing information about their profiles, purchasing habits and so forth.

The infomediary will be the agent of the consumer, putting their 'brand' equity before short-term exploitation. Once an infomediary has a very complete profile of a customer, it can add more value so that the customer does not tend to split his or her purchases between too many suppliers.

Amazon.com's '1-Click' is a simple example: it gets to know the customer's address, credit card details, shipping preferences and some of the customer's personal tastes about books and CDs. As the customer starts to buy gifts online using Amazon's new services, Amazon will accumulate knowledge about the birthdays and other anniversaries of the customer's family and friends. The company may choose (with the customer's permission) to remind the customer of special occasions in advance and to offer things it knows the customer likes to give as gifts, as well as reminding them of what was given last time and so on. Will that customer want to teach another service provider all that he or she taught Amazon? It seems unlikely. So, the more the customer teaches the agent, the more he or she has invested in the relationship, and the more the customer keeps teaching that agent, the more value he or she can get from the agent.

From a seller's perspective, if Amazon is the agent of choice for the majority of people in the seller's target group, the seller will be attracted to Amazon more than any other channel, and will offer the company special deals and

The device that is likely to change Internet access habits the most, however, is the mobile phone.

a high quality of service and be highly responsive to the chat room feedback from the Amazon community. The seller cannot hope to replicate the customer profile knowledge of Amazon, so it agrees to work with Amazon as its infomediary. Amazon can exploit this relationship to provide its customers with better offers. This, in turn, further enhances the consumer attractiveness of the infomediary.

The scramble for ownership of deep and broad consumer profiles will consolidate the market for infomediaries. There may even be a number of niche online communities for certain types of customer. Each niche community would know relatively little about its members, but would find it in the best interests of both parties (customer and niche infomediary) to join a larger confederation such as Amazon in order to provide better billing, book distribution, specialist video distribution and so on. The larger confederation may even find it worthwhile to pay the small infomediary to fall in under its umbrella. In turn, the large confederation learns yet more about its customers and can provide even more services to them. Therefore, it is possible to envisage the development of a few very big umbrella communities through which we will transact most of our online purchases (Hagel and Armstrong, 1997).

The way in which consumers will access the Internet is also changing. In particular, the emphasis is likely to shift in future away from the desktop or laptop PC as the sole means of Internet connection, towards other devices including palmtop computers, set top boxes, in-car computers that access traffic and weather information and provide satellite navigation, games machines and LCD projectors with built-in connectivity, and electronic schoolbooks. The device that is likely to change Internet access habits the most, however, is the mobile phone. Internet-enabled mobile phones can already handle voice, fax and e-mail transmissions. Companies such as 7/24 are working on mobiles that link to other customer services such as banking, and Orange has just introduced the first mobile videophone to use GSM.

A similar logic holds in business-to-business relationships where, arguably, the function of infomediaries is already established. This phenomenon is already appearing in the form of Internet-based exchanges and auctions such as Bartercard (http://www.bartercard.com). The next development is for brokers such as Charles Schwab and E*Offering (wholly owned by discount broker E*Trade) to offer complete share placings over the Internet. Not only would this be much cheaper for the companies floating on the stock market than the conventional underwriting route, it would also allow the use of auction techniques to prevent the underpricing not uncommonly associated with new issues, particularly of high-tech stocks (Tully, 1999).

The Internet seems to be one area in which major cost savings can be realised. Figure 4.3 illustrates the potential for reducing the cost of processing banking transactions via the Internet.

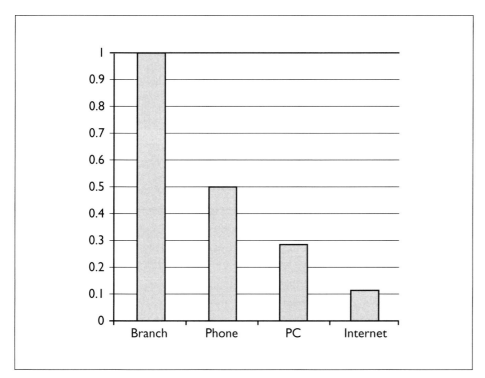

FIGURE 4.3

Retail banking unit transaction costs

(*Source:* de Kare-Silver, 1998)

The Internet has made a significant contribution to the financial services market. For example, whereas there were just sixty mortgage web sites four years ago, there were 3000 two years later (Harari, 1999). In 1995, Security First Network Bank opened its doors as the first Internet bank to offer customers full-service cheque accounts and banking services. This allowed customers to make automated funds transfer deposits, pay bills and reconcile their accounts. Another example is the use of the Web for customer support: a phone conversation may cost up to US$50, but support via the Web might cost only a few cents. Dataquest estimates that 60 per cent of customer support will be handled over the Internet by 2000, and the big ERP vendors are looking to become involved (Brooks, 1998). Microsoft claims that, although its web site costs $4 million per year to operate, it deflects calls that would cost an estimated $19 million per year to process in a call centre (Computer Sciences Corporation, 1998). The case of Cisco demonstrates the dramatic impact that the Internet can have upon the business model.

Case study ● **CISCO**

Cisco Systems, the international software company, took the decision to transfer more than 80 per cent of its help desk operation to the Web. Within 90 days of opening its support site the company was receiving almost 50 per cent of its contacts via the Internet. In an interesting variant on the 80/20 rule, just 20 developers handle more than 80 per cent of enquiries via the Web, yet it takes 800 engineers to deal with the remaining 20 per cent!

Through its web site, the company has cut the costs of paper catalogues, physical distribution of software and customer service, and has saved in excess of $500 million. Its web site accounts for $2 billion of sales per year.

One reason for Cisco's rapid growth is its development of a network of e-business partners, some of whom are simultaneously collaborating and competing ('coopetition'). Cisco has linked the other members of its supply chain directly to its web site, so that they receive immediate feedback about customer behaviour and needs.

(*Sources:* Court *et al.*, 1999; Jacobs *et al.*, 1999; Tapscott *et al.*, 1998)

Customer acquisition costs via web sites are much lower than by other means and one company, CyberGold, is exploiting this differential. The company pays consumers to visit its web site, which hosts adverts and surveys from a number of companies such as Disney and AT&T. Visitors to the site receive cash or discount vouchers for responding to questionnaires or adverts. CyberGold makes money by offering its corporate customers a 25 per cent discount on their existing customer acquisition costs and then pocketing the difference (Garber 1999).

Cisco is not the only company to make dramatic savings from web-based catalogues. Business-to-business web-based procurement offers the possibility of very significant savings, with online ordering costs perhaps one-tenth of the cost of processing a telephone order. SQL Financials International surveyed its customers and found that medium-sized business services companies could expect to save $250 to $500 per employee per year using online procurement. Larger companies with turnover in excess of $2 billion could achieve savings of up to $5000 per employee per year (Martin, 1999). The RS Components case study below illustrates how a win-win situation between customers and suppliers can be achieved in a business-to-business context:

Case study ● RS COMPONENTS

RS Components has spent £2.5 million on developing an Internet site, which was expected to attract less than 1 per cent of sales in 1999, a time when business-to-business electronic commerce in its main markets (the UK and the rest of Europe) was in its infancy. However, the decision to place the Internet at the heart of company strategy was an obvious move for the company that has prided itself on using technology to underpin its customer service.

An efficient ordering process lies at the heart of RS's business: some 130 000 different components are stocked, and its customers are typically engineers and small tradesmen who generally want quick delivery of small quantities. Typical orders are worth about £80, but these customers want availability, reliability, quality and technical support; price is fifth on their list of priorities.

In 1994, when RS was seeking a solution to the problem of handling its rapidly increasing product list, it decided to introduce CD-ROM catalogues which showed it how technology could shape its business. The next step, the introduction of an Internet site, appeared to offer potential solutions to some of RS's basic delivery problems, particularly its expanding catalogue. But RS also realised that it completely changed its relationship with its customers. The Chief Executive commented: '… it was not just a case of transferring the CD-ROM to the Net. We had to completely rethink the relationship …' The web site (http://rswww.com) and Internet strategy were developed in 18 months and won a commendation in the 1998 FT Web Site awards.

RS claims several advantages for its web site:

- A new ordering and distribution channel has reduced costs for the company in completing orders, and for customers in placing them. The cost to RS of completing a conventional order, from placement to payment of the invoice, is estimated at £60, but it is reduced to £10 using the Internet, which has produced savings of £100 000 in a year.

- The data gleaned has provided high quality information on customers. The company now knows the products that its customers buy and those that they do not, so it can start to address how to create value from this information.

- The site appeals to new customers, as one-third of the 50 000 registered site users are new. At present, there are ten customer categories, and the site channels users into areas of the catalogue likely to be of most interest to them. Ultimately, in the true sense of CRM, there will be a category for each individual customer.

- Customers are also attracted as a result of simply searching the Internet for a service such as that provided by RS. It is, therefore, inappropriate to judge the success of the site on the number of orders it produces, as many customers may be using the site for information purposes only and then placing orders by phone.

However, the power of the site is being limited by customers not being able to use it since many large companies in the UK refuse to trade electronically (only a quarter of RS's customers are registered users of the site). Nonetheless, RS is confident that this will change, bringing with it a change in the customer's relationship with RS. RS wishes to give its customers the power to search and shop around on the Internet, which will upset the traditional supplier–customer relationships in the market. RS aims to deliver a profitable service and to fulfil its customers' needs more effectively than the competition.

(*Source:* adapted from Price, 1999)

Figure 4.4 illustrates the hierarchy of connectivity that can be achieved between customer and supplier, and identifies the opportunities and challenges generated by e-business systems. The model has been adapted for use by Computer Sciences Corporation (1999a) to develop e-commerce capabilities among its clients.

FIGURE 4.4

The seven levels of interorganisational connectivity illustrate the opportunities and challenges of e-business

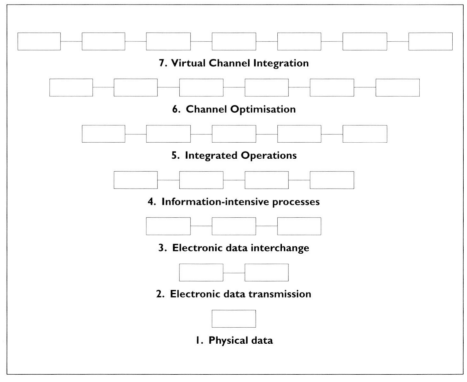

7. Virtual Channel Integration

6. Channel Optimisation

5. Integrated Operations

4. Information-intensive processes

3. Electronic data interchange

2. Electronic data transmission

1. Physical data

(*Source:* Computer Sciences Corporation, 1999a)

Level 1: Physical data transfer

- lowest and most traditional level of connectivity

- relies on direct physical transfer of information between channel members by mail or other manual means

- is clearly slow and labour-intensive for ordering

- has largely been replaced by some form of electronic order transmission.

Level 2: Electronic data transmission

- may not constitute a legal contract

- is more convenient than physical transfer

- is now the dominant means of exchanging information in many channels.

Level 3: Electronic data interchange

- EDI ordering eliminates several manual steps in the ordering process

- usage does not usually significantly increase interdependence within the channel

- adoption is justified primarily on ability to eliminate manual data-entry costs, and to increase order reliability and accuracy

- ordering is only faster if more EDI orders are able to bypass some steps of the less-automated phone or fax ordering process

- organisations adopt EDI because it is faster, more reliable and cheaper for the entire channel.

Level 4: New information-intensive processes and data transmission

- EDI is also used to exchange pricing changes, bill-back charges, advanced shipping notices, and other information related to invoicing and payment

- allows sharing of information that would probably not be shared in the absence of an infrastructure that makes transmissions almost automatic and free

- essentially manual processes are supplemented by process and technological innovations

- organisations adopt this level to expand availability of information and improve conflict resolution.

Level 5: New policies and integrated operations

- customers allow suppliers to ship products as needed to replenish inventory orders that might be paid for automatically when received, with a discount or float period negotiated as compensation for real-time payment

- represent new ways of supporting essential business activities for both customers and suppliers

- middle or senior managers from functional operations must become involved in the necessary investment and policy decisions

- organisations adopt this level to increase predictability and control channel processes.

Level 6: Joint channel optimisation relationships

- relationship moved beyond the ordering process to operations in general

- involves meetings and discussions between the businesses to improve the existing relationship

- a shift in perception of adjacent channel occupants from rivals to partners often emerges

- organisations adopt this level to invest in the relationship (even without short-term return, anticipating future opportunities to improve channel efficiency and effectiveness) to seek mutual gains.

Level 7: Virtual channel integration

- senior managers in both companies establish close relationships based on mutual trust

- both sides willing to disclose sensitive and proprietary information, such as information on costs, margins or plans for product introduction

- relationships regularly demand senior management attention to form and maintain the alliances

- partners should be chosen based on relationships gained at Level 6

- must be prepared to dissolve such relationships to make room for other, more fruitful partnerships.

From our survey of the literature about CRM, it is clear that CRM practitioners and researchers believe the implementation of CRM has consequences not just in the way organisations do business, but also in the way company information is handled. To gauge how far your company has come in building its CRM architecture, you may wish to complete the questionnaire in section 4.9.

4.9 EXERCISE: BUILDING YOUR CRM ARCHITECTURE

Against each question, tick one box on the right according to how strongly you agree or disagree.

	disagree strongly	disagree	neither agree nor disagree	agree	agree strongly
1. My organisation has a strong track record in the implementation of large-scale, technology-enabled change.	☐	☐	☐	☐	☐
2. The organisation is very much aligned behind the move to become customer-centric and this effort has the strong personal commitment of key board members.	☐	☐	☐	☐	☐
3. The individual solutions and initiatives throughout the company are being pulled together and coordinated by a team clearly responsible for customer management.	☐	☐	☐	☐	☐
4. The current systems in the company, both in the front- and back-offices, are not considered an insurmountable barrier to creating a customer-centric business.	☐	☐	☐	☐	☐
5. We have, or will soon have, a single logical entity that accumulates our customer knowledge and makes it readily available to the business in a form that is easy to use.	☐	☐	☐	☐	☐
6. All customer-facing employees across marketing, sales and customer service share a complete view of individual customers. This view is readily available at the point of customer contact.	☐	☐	☐	☐	☐
7. Learning from customer databases is available to the front-office at the point of customer contact.	☐	☐	☐	☐	☐
8. The front-office is seamlessly linked to the company's back-office fulfilment systems so that it can make promises to customers with respect to offer, price and timings of delivery.	☐	☐	☐	☐	☐
Now score each tick as shown:	1	2	3	4	5
Enter your score per column in each box	☐	☐	☐	☐	☐

Total score:

How does your organisation score?

Score 8–20

The implementation of CRM is not advanced in your organisation. Issues relate to alignment within the organisation, complex 'legacy' systems that are difficult and expensive to fix or an uncoordinated approach to the individual CRM initiatives. It is possible that managers are repeatedly asked to rework the CRM business case in order to shed more light on the issues. Anyone of these barriers can virtually halt progress and it will require a powerful executive sponsor to become personally involved to move the programme forward.

There are two halves to the CRM architecture: the ability to learn and interact with individual customers and the ability to create different customer solutions.

Score 21–31

The CRM programme may be stuck in 'no man's land'. Clearly there is progress but your business is not yet customer focused. The risk of not accelerating the programme may advantage your competitors, particularly the newly built organisations whose business models are dedicated to interactive customer relationships.

At this stage, one would expect the programme to have senior sponsorship and sufficient internal alignment, although that is not always the case. The problems of implementation can lie in a number of areas:

*   the organisation has been learning about its customers, but has not yet committed to doing things differently for them on the basis of learning. For example, the report discusses the issues around the return on data warehousing investments;

*   the operational capacity to customise is not great enough and developing it is proving more difficult than expected;

*   the culture of being in a service business is not yet fully developed;

*   existing IT systems cannot be made to work in this new environment and there is not yet sufficient will or need to tackle this problem;

*   CRM implementation is highly fragmented and decentralised, perhaps reflecting the organisation's business model. This makes it very difficult to integrate initiatives and develop one robust view of the customer that is available to all customer-facing people.

The problems associated with existing IT systems can prove difficult and sometimes there are very good reasons why an organisation cannot resolve them in the short term. For instance, recently, it is likely that IT resources have been badly stretched with the demands of Year 2000 compliance, EMU and ERP.

IT aside, the issues are management ones. There are two halves to the CRM architecture: the ability to learn and interact with individual customers and the ability to create different customer solutions corresponding to the different needs. Much of the publicity about CRM concerns the former. The new technologies of the Internet, call centres, sales force automation and data warehousing have changed the economics around one-to-one marketing. Developing the operational capability to create tailored customer solutions may not be getting sufficient attention, perhaps because it links back to process re-engineering and core competency development which may be seen as somewhat passé in the organisation.

Finally, there is the very substantial issue of implementing CRM in an organisation whose success has been built upon business unit autonomy and entrepreneurship. The organisation's entrepreneurs must accept that there is a compelling case for sharing customer data, harmonising the data collected and making their businesses more interoperable so that one business can make promises to the customer on behalf of the entire organisation.

Score 32–40

Your organisation is developing a significant capability in the area of CRM that could prove difficult for competitors to emulate. The management team is working to the one goal and there are no substantial barriers to progress. Moreover, your company is implementing best practice in CRM architecture by creating an intelligent, integrated front-office that can direct the company's operational systems towards meeting the needs of individual customers.

In the next chapter, we consider the organisational and cultural implications of adopting CRM systems strategically.

5

Organisational and cultural implications

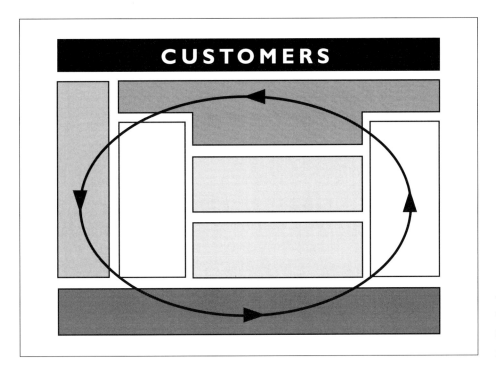

Even where organisations have integrated technologically, this does not always lead to performance integration.

Research by Computer Sciences Corporation (1998) suggests that organisations that have made technological investment but have not made the associated organisational changes have been disappointed with the results. By contrast, organisations that have adopted a balance of new technology and culture change have created strong, enduring and profitable customer relationships with a stable customer base.

Organisational and cultural factors are critical to the successful adoption of CRM. For example, the new wave of Enterprise Resource Planning (ERP) systems also offers systems that enable CRM. Having learned from the implementation difficulties in early ERP systems, these post-ERP systems will also address '... cultural and organisational shifts intended to align IT and business management objectives once and for all' (Stein and Caldwell, 1998). However, purchasers of the CRM software need to be aware that the vendors may be more keen to boost their diminishing ERP income by selling extended ERP capability than to meet their customers' needs for software to implement CRM (August, 1999).

5.1 ORGANISATIONAL INTEGRATION AND CRM METRICS

Hall (1997) finds that even where organisations have integrated technologically, this does not always lead to performance integration. He attaches great importance to the notion of aligning organisational goals and

IT systems, and argues that organisations should focus on how marketing and CRM can support performance throughout the entire organisation.

Lack of integration with other business systems is holding back the use of sales and marketing software; one survey found integration of the sales system with other business processes to be the highest priority sales and marketing investment over the following 18 months (Ferguson and Shaw, 1996).

However, it is not all down to business systems. Traditionally, a customer or key account manager would (and still does) play an important role in the customer relationship. The key to any successful implementation of CRM is an integrated approach within the organisation (Morris, 1994). Participation is required from people from marketing, quality management operations, market research, information technology, and financial accounting.

One change that organisations need to make is to set up customer focus teams or segment management groups to investigate and respond to the needs of specific customers or segments (Leuchter, 1997; Spitler, 1997). Although the ultimate goal may be the 'segment of one', where product/service offers are tailored specifically to the individual, this is not yet achievable in most companies. However, even realigning to serve a 'segment of several' requires cohesion between business units (Larson, 1996).

Developing teams is an approach supported by Monaghan (1995). Monaghan highlights the importance of customer management teams. On the upside, teams can:

- represent a way to align an organisation's functional resources with that of the customer
- increase the focus on the customer
- enhance flexibility
- bring a degree of functional expertise to the supplier-contact interface
- be a catalyst for change.

However, according to Monaghan there are drawbacks:

- teams are complex, thus expensive
- accountability can become diffused
- teams require special support, for example, sophisticated infrastructures
- teams are perhaps too customer-focused.

Any organisation needs to find the right balance. 'The effectiveness of any team will be affected by the way it is managed, trained, equipped, and directed' (Monaghan, 1995). Spitler (1997) would argue that the way the client team is measured is critical and is not currently well done: 'If there is a single shortfall today in the migration to a customer relationship model of the business, it is the lack of adequate, insightful customer MIS and customer performance metrics.'

Managing business processes has been a key area where organisations have undertaken initiatives to make improvements to the way they do business, particularly in dealing with customers. Some organisations have introduced performance measures to keep track of how well they are performing. One such measure is the Balanced Score Card, which provides management with a comprehensive framework in which to translate a company's strategic objectives into a coherent set of performance measures (Kaplan and Norton, 1993).

Jennings (1997) states that in order to successfully embrace customer scoring, the culture of the organisation will need to be adaptive and responsive to change. Once this culture is in place, customer scoring can be very beneficial for customer-oriented strategies.

5.2 SENIOR MANAGEMENT COMMITMENT

The success of any project will need commitment from the top. It is important that senior management show visible sponsorship and commitment to a customer relationship management initiative. Surveys undertaken by Martiny (1998) and Braganza and Myers (1996) highlight the importance of commitment by showing that respondents scored this as critical.

A META Group report (META Group, 1998) singled out CEO involvement as a critical success factor for CRM projects. META concluded that 'investing in CRM technology without a customer-oriented cultural mindset – inherited hierarchically throughout the enterprise from the CEO – is like throwing money into a black hole'. A recent survey undertaken in the USA by Exchange Applications found that many CEOs are making CRM a priority.

5.3 CONVERGENCE OF SYSTEMS

Elliott (1997) identifies that the convergence of disparate information systems will assist companies in the areas of cost reduction, improved efficiency and increased productivity. The process of convergence will accelerate the development of customer-serving processes and facilitate information sharing among employees.

5.4 EMPLOYEES: ROLE AND RECOGNITION

It is not just technology and process that can influence the customer relationship. People play just as important a part. The key is to organise employees around the customer.

The key is to organise around the customer.

When an employee comes into contact with a customer it is sometimes difficult to gauge the relationship and the degree of customer satisfaction. However, companies are far more likely to lose customers because of an attitude or indifference on the part of the company employee than because of a misunderstanding of customer needs (Galbreath, 1998).

In order to meet organisational challenges, marketing and technology skills will become increasingly important. It is critical that an organisation invests to develop and improve these skills. Elliott (1997) feels that some jobs will become obsolete as a result of IT executives not keeping up with the pace of change or resisting change.

It also important that an organisation maintains its competitive edge by constantly training employees, reinforcing existing procedures, and implementing newly created programmes (McDonald, 1993). At Dell, technicians are trained to hone the customer relationship skills they need for telephone support and problem guidance, and to focus directly on the customer's needs without using technical jargon. Ritz-Carlton combines employee training with information systems to provide its guests with superior service whenever they stay with the hotel chain.

Case study • RITZ-CARLTON

The Ritz-Carlton hotel chain trains its entire staff, from those on the front desk to those in maintenance and housekeeping, on how to converse with customers and how to handle complaints immediately. In addition, it provides each staff member with a 'guest preference pad' for recording every preference gleaned from conversations with and observations of customers. Every day, these preferences are entered on to a worldwide database. This could have benefits in the future. For example, if you call for room service in a hotel in Mexico and ask for an ice cube in your drink, months later, if you are staying in a Ritz-Carlton hotel in Spain and order a drink, the drink will come with an ice cube in it.

One area where employees can be encouraged to show greater commitment to the customer relationship is through recognition and reward. For example, if an employee receives a complimentary letter from a customer, then he or she can be rewarded by the company in some way. Also, allowing the employee a certain degree of autonomy when dealing with the customer is a recognition of their competence.

5.5 CUSTOMERS

As well as addressing internal organisational and cultural issues, firms assembling electronic databases need to address the concerns of their customers.

Investments in CRM allow companies to work 'smarter, not harder'. Offering customers additional products that are of interest and relevance to them benefits the customer as well as the organisation making the offer. Increased response rates to direct mail campaigns is one of the most striking and measurable impacts of CRM investment. Greater targeting in marketing campaigns also reduces the irritation factor for the customer, who may otherwise be deluged with what he or she regards as junk mail. McKean (1999) cites one US investment brokerage with an aggressive approach to direct marketing. If a customer of this brokerage had four products and performed at least one transaction per annum, they were likely to receive 160 unsolicited mailings! This particular firm had to change its attitude about marketing to customers; it also invested $4 million in improved information systems, which made marketing campaigns so much more successful that the cost was recouped within a year (McKean, 1999).

As well as addressing internal organisational and cultural issues, firms assembling electronic databases need to address the concerns of their customers. They must engender trust among users of their web sites and others who provide them with data so that they feel comfortable that their privacy and security has been protected (Computer Sciences Corporation,

1999a). Hagel and Rayport (1997) suggest that many privacy concerns may be attributed to the perceived value exchanged by the user with the organisation collecting the data.

Where both customers and suppliers believe that they receive value from a closer relationship, the rewards can be considerable. A study of relationship marketing in the automotive industry found that customers were far more supportive of their suppliers if the supplier pursued a relational marketing policy, and were far more likely to reciprocate with a relational approach to purchasing. These results are particularly striking in an industry where there are major size differences and hence power differences between suppliers and customers (Brennan, 1999).

Where both customers and suppliers believe that they receive value from a closer relationship, the rewards can be considerable.

5.6 RESISTANCE TO CHANGE, AND CRM FAILURES

Although there is an enthusiasm for using IT, nearly 80 per cent of sales and marketing professionals in the survey conducted by Softworld (1998) said that there is a gap between what IT should be able to provide to Sales and Marketing, and what it is actually delivering. Integrating new technology into existing systems was cited as the main difficulty. A number of additional barriers to the adoption of IT systems remain: lack of clear strategy, budgetary constraints, lengthy implementation times, resistance to change, and lack of user knowledge and specialist training (Littlewood, 1999). Within the insurance industry the Swiss insurer, Winterthur, found that it took years to convince the company's captive agents that centralising customer data and creating a multi-channel distribution network would increase their own profitability (Curley, 1999).

Leverick *et al.* (1998) cite a series of studies concerning the success or failure of IT installations. One survey of 400 British and Irish companies found that only 11 per cent of respondents said their installation had been successful. Another study found that 30–40 per cent of IT projects realise no appreciable benefits at all. A third study found that three-quarters of IT projects were either uncompleted or not used when they were completed. Four success criteria were cited in the research: scope of applications, perceived benefits achieved, project completion on time, and return on investment. Pitt *et al.* (1995) cite research by Laudon and Laudon (1991) showing IS failure rates of between 35 per cent and 75 per cent. The Sistrum CRM Group (1999a) estimates that between 50 per cent and 60 per cent of current CRM projects will not give real business benefits, with international projects particularly likely to fail.

Sistrum (1999b) discusses three approaches to CRM projects: Big Bang, Tactical Initiatives, and Green Field. Big Bang projects are single, large CRM projects, often rolled out internationally, and involving changes in processes and culture. They offer the possibility of capturing economies of scale, but are seen as high risk and slow. Tactical Initiatives are local systems such as sales force support that are lower cost and offer quick wins, but they can be difficult to scale up. Green Field initiatives are about rapid introduction of new channels such as call centres or e-commerce. These, however, can turn out to be very costly ways of acquiring and servicing unprofitable customers. Sistrum suggests that the best route is in fact an incremental approach in which a planned series of projects is rolled out across the organisation, with clear objectives and priorities. This helps to avoid 'scope creep' and unrealistic timescales, which are key reasons for failure, while offering the prospect of some early wins (Sistrum, 1999b).

A customer survey conducted by CRM software specialist Hatton Blue indicated that 39 per cent of clients perceived the length of implementation as being a major inhibiting factor to success, while 35 per cent named cultural issues and the pressure to complete other IT projects, and 34 per cent cited the difficulty of integrating technologies (Reed, 1999).

Saunders (1999) draws attention to a report by Ovum Inc. warning that CRM software can be deficient in terms of cross-channel support. For example, a product may perform well in call centres, but it may be inadequate at supporting Web or other media used to contact customers or sales agents.

The quality of communication within an organisation is an important aspect of any change initiative. Failing to successfully communicate a change initiative and its implications could lead to failure. Thus, an effective internal communication strategy needs to be in place, so employees can 'buy-in' to the initiative.

In chapter 6, we summarise the key findings of our survey of CRM and consider the future of CRM.

Failing to successfully communicate a change initiative and its implications could lead to failure.

6

Summary and trends

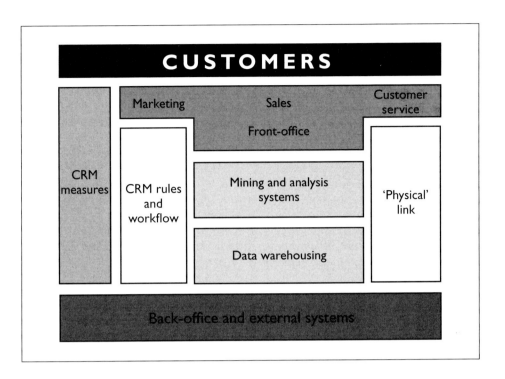

In this chapter, we put our 'road map' of CRM back together and consider the current state of CRM and possible future developments. Our conclusions are as follows:

CRM is a significant management issue. The number of articles about CRM found by one database search increased from five in 1991 to 2388 seven years later, the majority of which were published in the USA. Customer profitability also increased in importance as a topic, from one article in 1993 to 100 in the same time period. Our search has identified the relatively advanced position of the financial services industry. Under CRM, banking was one of the top 20 key words; in a search combining CRM and customer profitability, it occurred three times in the top 12 terms. *American Banker* was the fourth most prolific publisher of CRM articles and *Bank Marketing* the twelfth. In contrast, the most prolific marketing publication was *Sales and Marketing Management*, which was ranked fourteenth.

Supplying CRM systems is now a hugely competitive industry. There have been a number of new developments within the last few years.

- In March 2000, E-Gain Communications announced a merger with Inference Corp to give both partners critical mass in the CRM market.

- In February 2000, two CRM-based mergers were announced. i2 Technologies said it would acquire Aspect Development and E.piphany Inc announced a $3.2billion bid for Octane Software.

A key driver of the trend towards consolidation will be the demand for integrated, organisation-wide systems.

- In September 1999, SAP announced mySAP, an e-business add-on to its ERP system, in response to customer pressure for CRM capability on their SAP systems.

- In April 1998, NCR announced it would deliver industry-specific customer relationship management programmes.

- In July 1998, Broadbase Information Systems announced that one of the US leading banks, BankBoston, had deployed Broadbase software solutions to analyse customer trends, optimise marketing activities, and improve customer loyalty within its credit card marketing group.

- In August 1998, IBM created an autonomous software unit dedicated to CRM, identifying CRM as a key area where IBM will apply its expertise.

- In October 1998, the SAS Institute announced strategic sales to leading organisations during the third quarter of its fiscal year. Key technologies driving these sales were data warehousing and customer relationship management.

- In November 1998, Oracle announced that its profitability solution, which is based on Oracle® Performance Analyzer and Oracle Transfer Pricing, is now being used by over thirty financial services firms around the world.

- In December 1998, Prism Solutions introduced an application called Campaign Advisor, a full-featured market analysis and campaign management solution designed to help financial services organisations identify, build and retain their most profitable customers.

Technology plays a central role in successful CRM projects. There are now a significant number of suppliers of CRM products and systems in the market. The recent trend has been towards consolidation, through acquisition and alliances, and this is likely to continue. A key driver of the trend towards consolidation will be the demand for integrated, organisation-wide systems and 'the elimination of any division of the front and back offices' (Dawes and Rowley, 1998).

For the purchasers of CRM systems, however, it is not just a technology issue. CRM raises significant organisational issues, such as culture and employee attitudes towards customers; these will become even more critical as CRM technologies become integrated and are no longer designed around isolated initiatives owned by a single department. The ultimate objective is greater flexibility and responsiveness to customers – not 'piecemeal automation' that leaves organisations 'technologically muscle-bound' (Adolf and Hooda, 1997). Discussing the banking industry in the

1980s and early 1990s, and the declining share of traditional institutions, they comment: 'As new players took market share using new strategies and technologies, they drove home a brutal truth – in a fast-evolving market, combining and automating discrete processes and products is insufficient to win and retain customers.'

Customers are assets with legs – they can walk away.

Increasingly, CRM will be seen as a company-wide initiative that demands integration between departments and systems – or even integration beyond the traditional organisational boundary in partnerships and networks (Webster, 1992). At the moment, there is a war going on in many organisations over who has responsibility for information – IT, marketing or finance (Curran, 1998). Until these turf wars are resolved, internal wrangling can damage an organisation's ability to compete. Companies need to keep pace with increasing user access, through specialist marketing departments and integrated enterprise-wide technology.

Another feature of the adoption of CRM is that customers are helping to drive change and are demanding greater participation (Martin, 1999; Dawes and Rowley, 1998). Customers are assets with legs – they can walk away. A customer orientation will become increasingly recognised as a source of competitive advantage, and customer-oriented organisations will strive to recognise customer differences, enable two-way communications, and aim to educate and inform customers (Nwankwo, 1995). The attitude of employees in all of this is vital; superior performance can be completely negated in the customer's eyes by poor service and employee attitude (Nwankwo, 1995).

6.1 THE FUTURE OF CRM

So, what of the future? CRM is likely to gather pace in the next few years, and there is still scope for new and better products and services. Michael de Kare-Silver (1998) predicts some major developments as early as 2005. Citing sources about the degree of connectivity, he points out that by the end of 2000, some 40 per cent of US and 20 per cent of UK and German households will have Net access. By 2002, 30 per cent of households in the major Asian economies will also be connected. He predicts that there will be an explosion in e-commerce, and that traditional retailers will find themselves in difficulties: 'Already about 15–20 per cent of consumers say they'd prefer to shop electronically rather than visiting the shops. It only takes a drop of 15 per cent in store traffic to make many stores unprofitable' (op. cit., p. 8). Direct retailing could constitute 55 per cent of

CRM will not just 'go away'; it is not just the latest management buzzword.

the market by 2010, and it has been predicted that physical shops could eventually become a thing of the past. And how many retailers would be prepared to take the dramatic step taken by US software retailer Egghead? In the face of growing competition from computer superstores, Egghead closed all its 80 stores, laid off 80 per cent of its workers, and focused on selling via the Internet. The company saved $20 million per year and now trades successfully as Egghead.com (Martin, 1999).

CRM is an inevitable development from the adoption of relationship marketing in organisations.

6.2 CONCLUSIONS

All the signs are that CRM will not just 'go away'; it is not just the latest management buzzword or business school fad. Organisations are already investing millions of dollars in CRM systems. The impetus behind the adoption of CRM is coming from managers who believe that the benefits their companies will obtain from better customer information and the ability to provide better service levels to their customers will translate into substantially higher profits in the future.

CRM is a strategic investment.

With the benefit of hindsight, CRM is an inevitable development from the adoption of relationship marketing in organisations, and the information and communications requirements this entails. Relationship marketing has as its emphasis on both getting *and keeping* customers. This means managing the relationship with the customer as a business asset, including investing in the relationship for the future. The shift to a relationship marketing philosophy has been the first key driver for CRM adoption. An important aspect of the shift to relationship marketing is in high-level buy-in; the support of the CEO is critical. The second key driver has been the availability of the technology. Technology now exists that enables organisations to offer significantly higher levels of service than hitherto. Companies can use data mining, not just to become informed about customers' previously expressed preferences, but also to identify potential customer needs – perhaps even before customers themselves are aware of them.

In the future we will see more sophisticated enterprise-wide CRM systems.

Another sign that CRM is a strategic investment is the way that many of the actions relating to CRM are fundamentally changing the way organisations work. Managing the customer relationship is a process that runs across departmental boundaries. It is noticeable that cross-functional working is a feature of successful CRM. Moreover, it has been suggested that the role of the customer will become much more active in the digital economy, and that connected companies may work with their customers in a collaborative 'sense and respond' approach, rather than the traditional 'make and sell' business model (Barabba in Tapscott *et al.*, 1998).

Pressure to adopt CRM will also come from customers.

It is likely that in the future we will see more widespread adoption of CRM and also of more sophisticated enterprise-wide CRM systems. As organisations become more confident in their use of CRM technology, they are likely to invest in increasingly complex, integrated CRM systems. This has an immediate consequence; these large CRM systems make expensive investments and their payback is more difficult to determine than smaller, specific applications. To isolate and measure the short-term profit impact of a campaign management system is comparatively straightforward; however, measuring the payback on a massive investment in data warehousing aimed at increasing overall customer service levels is much more complicated. At present, many of these very large investments take place without a proper business case in place. This will need to change as more and more companies move to integrated CRM.

Pressure to adopt CRM will also come from customers who experience the benefits of dealing with organisations that use technology to improve service levels. Changes in customer expectations will increasingly drive service levels and demand CRM capability. One example of this has been developments in inbound call centres. Already, mail-order customers telephoning call centres expect to give no more than their postcode, rather than the whole address. Very soon, customers will expect calling line identification linked to a data warehouse so that the call centre operator will already have the customer details on-screen when he or she picks up the telephone. The same is true in financial services, where it is companies such as First Direct and Direct Line who are setting service standards in their industry through their use of technology. The expectations of car buyers are also changing with the advent of interactive digital TV as an information and sales medium and the use of CD-ROMs to offer virtual test drives (Stone and Cerasale, 1999).

Customers may in future use fewer suppliers to supply a higher proportion of their needs.

A possible consequence is that customers may in future use fewer suppliers to supply a higher proportion of their needs. There are signs of this already in food retailing, where the major players have increased their share of customer spend and are branching out into petrol, pharmacy, clothing and financial services. Customer loyalty and patience with non-performing suppliers will further reduce, opening up possibilities of increased competition from outside a supplier's industry sector and from overseas. Both food retailing and financial services have already experienced this phenomenon. Companies without CRM capability will be at a serious competitive disadvantage.

This review of the CRM literature demonstrates that there is no generally accepted model for building the business case. CRM developments have been practitioner-led, with a focus on implementation rather than justification. The lack of a business model (a methodology for developing the business case) means that it may be difficult for organisations to justify major investments in CRM systems. This is likely to be a considerable danger where results are harder to measure, as in larger integrative investments such as data warehouses. Organisations may find it easier to approve limited investments in discrete systems such as campaign management, simply because the business case is more straightforward. These linked investments may offer short-term wins but fail to address some of the fundamental long-term business issues. There may also be a tendency to overestimate the returns on campaign management software because the success of such software may be dependent upon a data warehouse, the cost of which is not factored into the payback calculation.

The consequences for companies lacking a clear business case for long-term CRM investments are twofold. For those delaying CRM investments, service to customers will be slow to improve and certain customer service innovations that depend on investment in call centres, data warehousing or e-commerce may never be realised. Such organisations will also lose the competitive edge that knowledge of customers and a better understanding of their needs can give them in anticipating and adapting to market trends.

The growing pressure on organisations to make substantial investments in large CRM systems will result in CEOs demanding hard and soft information about the payback on CRM. However, measuring the payback on an integrated CRM system that increases the overall service levels across the organisation is difficult. The kind of measurement that has been used to date – usually the return on investment on discrete software tools which improve the efficiency of specific marketing processes such as campaign management – will not be appropriate because it is too limited. Major CRM investments should be measured on their ability to create longer-term value, not short-term profit or return on investment. Moreover, CRM is about helping companies to focus on customers, not products. Therefore, the appropriate metric for evaluating an investment in CRM is the impact that is has on the value of the customer. It is likely that the business case for CRM investments will in future be based on the resultant increase in the total value of the individual customer over the lifetime of the relationship.

Bibliography

Adolf, R. and Hooda, R. (1997) 'Customer-centric technology', *Banking Strategies*, 73 (6), 38–44.

Adolf, R., Grant-Thompson, S., Harrington, W. and Singer, M. (1997) 'What leading banks are learning about big databases and marketing', *The McKinsey Quarterly*, 3, 187–92.

American Banker (editorial) (1998) 'Customer Relationship Management: how can banks regain foothold with consumers in today's world?', *American Banker*, 163 (218), 13 November.

American Banker interview (1995) 'Q: How do banks stand to benefit most from improved segmentation of their customer base?' *American Banker*, 160 (141), 14.

Anton, J. (1996) *Customer Relationship Management: Making Hard Decisions with Soft Numbers*. New Jersey: Prentice-Hall.

Anton, J., Perkins, D.S. and Monger, J. (1995) 'Measuring customer satisfaction, *Telemarketing*, 14 (2), 90–5.

August, V. (1999) 'Escape modules', *Informationweek*, 61, 36–8.

Axson, D.A.J. (1992) 'A return to managing customer relationships', *International Journal of Bank Marketing*, 10 (1), 30–5.

Baker, S. and Baker, K. (1998) 'Mine over matter', *Journal of Business Strategy*, 19 (4), 22–6.

Battles, B.E., Mark, D. and Ryan, C. (1993) 'How otherwise good managers spend too much on information technology', *The McKinsey Quarterly*, 96 (3), 117–27.

Beckett-Camarata, E.J., Camarata, M.R. and Barker, R.T. (1998) 'Integrating internal and external customer relationships through relationship management: a strategic response to a changing global environment', *Journal of Business Research*, 41 (1), 71–81.

Belfer, S. (1998) 'IT are from Mars, and marketing are from Venus', *Direct Marketing*, 61 (5), 52–4.

Bennett, R. (1992) 'Gaining a competitive advantage through customer satisfaction', *Bank Marketing*, 24 (12), 24–6.

Berkley, B.J. and Gupta, A. (1994) 'Improving service quality with information technology', *International Journal of Information Management*, 14 (2), 109–21.

Bessen, J. (1993) 'Riding the marketing information wave', *Harvard Business Review*, 71 (5), 150–60.

Braganza, A. and Myers, A. (1996) 'Issues and dilemmas facing organisations in the effective implementation of BPR', *Business Change and Re-engineering*, 13 (2).

Brennan, R. (1999) 'Relationship management in the automotive industry, *International Journal of Customer Relationship Management*, 1 (4).

Britt, F.F. (1998) 'Customer leverage', *Progressive Grocer*, 77 (9), 44.

Broady-Preston, J. and Hayward, T.E. (1998), 'An assessment of the relationship between marketing, information and strategy formulation in the UK retail banking sector', *International Journal of Information Management*, 18 (4), 277–85.

Brooks, A. (1998) 'More satisfied customers, more satisfying returns', *Computing Canada*, 24 (38), 29.

Brown, S.A. (1996) 'Technology and customer satisfaction: myths and facts', *Canadian Business Review*, 23 (2), 29-31.

Campbell, N.C.G. and Cunningham, M.T. (1990) 'Customer analysis for strategy development in industrial markets', in Ford, D. (ed), *Understanding Business Markets: Interaction, Relationships, Networks.* London: Academic Press.

Carroll, P. and Tadikonda, M. (1997) 'Customer profitability: irrelevant for decisions?', *Banking Strategies*, 73 (6), 76–80.

Cesare, M-C. and Salaun, Y. (1995) 'Information and total relational gains', *International Journal of Information Management*, 15 (3), 209–22.

Codington, S. and Wilson, T. (1994) 'Information systems in the UK insurance industry', *International Journal of Information Management*, 14 (3), 188–203.

Colkin, E. (1999) 'Customer relationships get smarter', *Informationweek*, 738, 34.

Computer Sciences Corporation (1998) *Deploying Systems at the Customer Interface*, Foundation Operational Excellence report published by CSC.

Computer Sciences Corporation (1999a) *Developing an Electronic-commerce Capability*, Foundation Strategic Innovation report published by CSC.

Computer Sciences Corporation (1999b) *Deploying Systems at the Customer Interface: Future Trends in Customer Relationship Management*, Technology Study Tour report published by CSC.

Connolly, T. and Ashworth, G. (1994) 'Managing customers for profit', *Management Accounting*, 72 (4), 34–9.

Corss, R. and Smith, J. (1995) 'Customer bonding and the information core', *Direct Marketing*, 57 (10), 28–31.

Couldwell, C. (1998) 'A data day battle', *Computing*, 64–6.

Couldwell, C. (1999) 'Loyalty bonuses', *Marketing Week*, 18 February.

Court, D., French, T.D., McGuire, T.I. and Partington, M. (1999) 'Marketing in 3-D', *McKinsey Quarterly*, 4.

Cravens, D.W., Greenley, G., Piercy, N.F. and Slater, S.F. (1998) 'Mapping the path to market leadership: effectively combining various dimensions of strategy into an integrated process of strategic analysis and action maps the path to market leadeship', *Marketing Management*, 7 (3), 28–39.

Credit Card Management (1998) Top 10 Technologies Supplement, 26–31.

Culnan, M.J. (1995) 'Fair game or fair play? Corporations, to keep their customers, need to balance the power of information with privacy', *Journal of Business Strategy*, 16 (6), 29–31.

Curley, B. (1999) 'Profiting from the relationship', *Insurance & Technology*, 24 (3), 34–8.

Curran, P.J. (1998) 'Turning information into knowledge for competitive advantage: according to a report published this month, finance, IT and marketing departments in many organisations are fighting one another for responsibility to manage the company's information, *Management Accounting*, 76 (4), 26–7.

Dawes, J. and Rowley, J. (1998) 'Enhancing the customer experience: contributions from information technology', *Management Decision*, 36 (5), 350–7.

de Kare-Silver, M. (1997) *Strategy in Crisis*. London: Macmillan.

de Kare-Silver, M. (1998) *e-shock*. London: Macmillan Business.

Deighton, J. (1996) 'The future of interactive marketing', *Harvard Business Review*, vol. 74, no. 6, 151–60.

Desai, C., Wright, G. and Fletcher, K. (1998) 'Barriers to successful implementation of database marketing: a cross-industry study', *International Journal of Information Management*, 18 (4), 265–75.

Disney, D.R. (1995) 'For the real gold in customer data, dig deep', *American Banker*, 160 (89), 15.

Domegan, C.T. (1996) 'The adoption of information technology in customer service', *European Journal of Marketing*, vol. 30, no. 6, 52–69.

Dorman, J. and Hasan, M. (1996) 'Turning lead into gold', *Bank Marketing*, 28 (11), 28–32.

Duboff, R.S. (1992) 'Segmenting your market: marketing to maximize profitability', *Journal of Business Strategy*, 13 (6), 10.

Economist Intelligence Unit (1998) 'Managing customer relationships', The Economist Intelligence Unit, report with Andersen Consulting.

Elliott, C. (1997) 'Everything wired must converge', *Journal of Business Strategy*, 18 (6), 30–4.

Ernst and Young (1999) *Technology in Financial Services*, Special Report.

Evans, R.H. (1996) 'Mining gold in the mountains of customer data', *American Banker*, 161 (58), 19.

Fabris, P. (1998) 'Advanced navigation', *CIO*, 11 (15), 50–5.

Feldman, J. M. (1999) 'Marketing one-to-one', *Air Transport World*, 36 (7), 35.

Ferguson, N. and Shaw, A. (1996) 'Alone and unloved', *Conspectus*, November.

Fletcher, K. (1999) 'Data focus on customers', *Marketing*, 11 March, 52–3.

Fletcher, K. and Wright, G. (1995) 'Organizational, strategic and technical barriers to successful implementation of database marketing', *International Journal of Information Management*, 15 (2), 115–26.

Fletcher, K. and Wright, G. (1996) 'The strategic context for information systems use: an empirical study of the financial services industry', *International Journal of Information Management*, 16 (2), 119–31.

Fletcher, K. and Wright, G. (1997) 'Strategic and organizational determinants of information system sophistication: an analysis of the uptake of database marketing in the financial services industry', *European Journal of Information Systems*, 6 (3), 141–54.

Foley, J. (1997) 'Market of one: ready, aim, sell!', *InformationWeek*, 618, 34–44.

Foley and Russell (1998) 'Mining your own business', *Information Week*, 673, 18–20.

Ford, D. (ed.) (1990) *Understanding Business Markets*. London: Academic Press.

Forsyth, R. (1999) 'Implementing customer relationship management systems in retail financial services: Banco Hispano case study', *International Journal of Customer Relationship Management*, 2 (1).

Fuglseth, A.M. and Gronhaug, K. (1994) 'Information systems as a secondary strategic resource: the case of bank credit evaluations', *International Journal of Information Management*, 14 (4), 269.

Galbreath, J. (1998) 'Relationship management environments', *Credit World*, 87 (2), 14–21.

Gamble, P.R., Stone, M. and Woodcock, N. (1999) *Up Close and Personal? Customer Relationship Marketing @ Work*. London: Kogan Page and New York: Dover.

Garber, J.R. (1999) 'Show me the money', *Forbes Global Business & Finance*, 8 March.

Gerson, V. (1998) 'Right on target', *Bank Marketing*, 30 (3), 24–8.

Gervino, J. (1998) 'Mining for gold in a data warehouse', *Bank Marketing*, 30 (5).

Glazer, R. (1997) 'Strategy and structure in information-intensive markets: the relationship between marketing and IT', *Journal of Market Focused Management*, 65–81.

Goebel, D.J., Marshall, G.W. and Locander, W.B. (1998) 'Activity-based costing: accounting for a market orientation', *Industrial Marketing Management*, 27 (6), 497–510.

Grant, A.W.H. and Schlesinger, L.A. (1995) 'Realize your customers' full potential', *Harvard Business Review*, 75 (5), 14.

Groenfeldt, T. (1997) 'Just like starting over', *Journal of Business Strategy*, 18 (3), 16–22.

Gronroos, C. (1996) 'Relationship marketing: strategic and tactical implications', *Management Decision*, 34 (3), 5–14.

Haapaniemi, P. (1996) 'Cyber-strategy', *Journal of Business Strategy*, 17 (1), 22–6.

Hagel, J., Bergsma, E.E. and Dheer, S. (1996) 'Placing your bets on electronic networks', *The McKinsey Quarterly*, 2, 56–67.

Hagel, J. and Armstrong, A.G. (1997) *Net gain: expanding markets through virtual communities*. Cambridge: Harvard Business School Press.

Hagel, J. and Rayport, J.F. (1997) 'Selling your privacy', *The Futurist*, 31(6), 15.

Hagel, J. and Sacconaghi, A.M. (1996) 'Who will benefit from virtual information?', *The McKinsey Quarterly*, 3, 22–37.

Hagel, J. and Singer, M. (1999) 'Unbundling the corporation', *Harvard Business Review*, 77 (2), 133.

Hall, D. (1997) 'Computerisation – where's the return on investment', *Management Accounting*, 75 (6), 40–1.

Hall, R. (1999) 'Practice makes perfect – not the other way around', *Bank Marketing*, 31 (1), 16.

Hallberg, G. (1995) *All Consumers are not Created Equal*, New York: Wiley.

Halper, M. (1996) 'Welcome to the 21st-century data', *Forbes*, 157 (7), 48–57.

Hansotia, B. (1996) 'Achieving world-class database marketing with customer-focused strategies', *Direct Marketing*, 59 (7), 58–60.

Harari, O. (1999) 'Obsolete.com?', *Management Review*, September, 31.

Harrison, J.J. (1993) 'Transforming data into relationships', *National Underwriter Life and Health – Financial Services Edition*, no. 31, 7–8.

Haynes, P.J., Helms, M.M. and Casavant Jnr, R. (1992) 'Creating a value-added customer database: improving marketing management decisions', *Market Intelligence & Planning*, 10 (1), 16–20.

Heasley, P.G. and Gross, P.W. (1997) 'Getting the most out of customer information', *Chief Executive* (US), 130, 36–9.

Hiss, R.G. (1999) 'Gaining an edge and keeping it with customer relationship management', *Siebel Magazine*, 2 (1).

Hoard, B. (1999) 'Caring for the customer', *Inform, Summer Supplement: Strategic Vision*, 19–23.

Hobby, J. (1999) 'Looking after the one who matters', *Accountancy Age*, 28 October, 28–30.

Insurance Systems Bulletin (1993) 'Customer service makes conflicting demands on IT,' *Insurance Systems Bulletin*, 9(4), 6–7.

Jacobs, M. (1999) 'Managing profitable customer relations in the new economy', *International Journal of Customer Relationship Management*, 2 (3).

Jennings, A. (1997) 'Customer relationship management using customer scoring', *Credit Management*, 30–2.

Jiang, J.J., Klein, G., Motwani, J. and Balloun, J. (1997) 'An investigation of marketing managers' dissatisfaction with marketing information systems', *International Journal of Information Management*, 17 (2), 115–21.

Johnson, B.A., Ott, J.H., Stephenson, J.M. and Weberg, P.K. (1995) 'Banking on multimedia', *The McKinsey Quarterly*, 95 (2), 95–107.

Kaplan, R.S. and Norton, D.P. (1993) 'Putting the balanced scorecard to work', *Harvard Business Review*, 71 (5), 134–42.

Kelly, S. (1996) 'Using data to optimise profitability and enable diversification', *Business Impact*, 7, 13–14.

Kelly, S. (1997), *Data Warehousing in Action*. New York: Wiley.

Kelly, S. and Boon, C. (1996) Kick starting the data warehouse, data warehouse network, *monograph*.

Kessler, A.J. (1997) 'The database economy', *Forbes*, 159 (8), 168.

Kiesnoski, K. (1999) 'Reining in information', *Bank Systems & Technology*, 36 (7), 32–3.

Kilbane, D. (1998) 'Analyze data for a better bottom line', *Automatic ID News*, 14 (10), 60–2.

Krupnicki, M. and Tyson, T. (1997) 'Using ABC to determine the cost of servicing customers', *Management Accounting*, 79 (6), 40–5.

Kutner, S. and Cripps, J. (1997) 'Managing the customer portfolio of healthcare enterprises', *The Healthcare Forum Journal*, 40 (5), 52–4.

Landberg, S.M. (1998) 'Taking advantage of convergence', *National Underwriter (Property & Casualty/Risk & Benefits Management)*, 102 (39), 59–61.

Larson, M. (1996) 'In pursuit of a lasting relationship', *Journal of Business Strategy*, 17(6), 31–3.

Laudon, K.C. and Laudon, J.P. (1991) *Management Information Systems: A Contemporary Perspective*. 2nd edn. New York: Macmillan.

Leuchter, M. (1997) 'Meaningful relationships (panel discussion)', *Journal of Business Strategy*, 18 (3), 42–6.

Leverick, F., Littler, D., Bruce, M. and Wilson, D. (1998) 'Using information technology effectively: a study of marketing installations', *Journal of Marketing Management*, 14 (8), 927–62.

Levitin, A.V. and Redman, T.C. (1998) 'Data as a resource: properties, implications, and prescriptions', *Sloan Management Review*, 40 (1), 89–102.

Lewington, J., de Chernatony, L. and Brown, A. (1996) 'Harnessing the power of database marketing', *Journal of Marketing Management*, 12, 329–46.

Littlewood, F. (1999) 'Driven by technology', *Marketing*, 11 March, 29–31.

Lockard, M. (1998) 'Test your retention IQ', *Target Marketing*, 21 (3), 32–41.

Maglitta, J.E. (1997) 'Beyond ROI', *Computerworld*, 3 (43), 73–4.

Makos, R. (1995) 'Decision support: harnessing the value of information', *Bank Management*, 71 (5), 73–5.

Management Today (1994) 'How to transform marketing through IT', *Special Report, Business Intelligence*.

Manchester, P. (1998) 'Customers in sharper focus', *Financial Times*, 2 September.

Mann, D.C. (1990) 'Database marketing, how it's changing your business', *Bank Marketing*, 22 (8), 30–4.

Martin, C. (1999) *Net Future*. New York: McGraw-Hill.

Martiny, M. (1998) 'Knowledge management at HP consulting', *Organizational Dynamics*, 27 (2), 71–7.

Mazur, L. (1993) 'Tools of the trade', *Marketing Business*, March, 23–8.

MCA (1999) *The Development of the Internet and the Growth of e-commerce*, Report by the Management Consultancies Association, London.

McDonald, L. (1993) 'Setting new standards for customer advocacy', *Journal of Business Strategy*, 14 (1), 11–15.

McDonald, M. and Wilson, H. (1999) 'e-marketing: improving marketing effectiveness in a digital world', FT Report. London: Financial Times Prentice Hall.

McKean, J. (1999) *Information Masters*. Chichester and New York: Wiley.

McKendrick, J. (1995) 'NGS responds to millions of queries', *Midrange Systems*, 8 (19), 3.

McKim, R. (1998) 'Facing technology head-on', *Target Marketing*, 21 (3), 58–60.

Meredith, S. (1996) 'Mind the gap', *Marketing Business*, November, 45–9.

META Group (1998), *The Seven Deadly Sins of CRM Implementation*, META Group Report, November.

Mitchell, A. (1997) 'Swimming with the sharks', *Marketing Business*, September.

Mitchell, A. (1998) 'Why intimacy is vital to customer relationships', *Marketing Week*, 21 (37), 30–1.

Monaghan, R. (1995) 'Customer management teams are here to stay', *Marketing News*, 29 (23).

Morris, T. (1994) 'Customer relationship management', *CMA Magazine*, 68 (7), 22–5.

Mullin, R. (1997) 'Taking customer relations to the next level', *Journal of Business Strategy*, 18 (1), 22–6.

Naval, M. (1998) 'Businesses missing the info advantage', *Computing Canada*, 24 (20), 13–15.

Neil, S. (1998) 'How to peek into the mind of a customer', *PC Week*, 15 (39), 73.

Nwankwo, S. (1995) 'Developing a customer orientation', *Journal of Consumer Marketing*, 12 (5), 5–15.

Orenstein, A.F. (1997) 'Putting information to work', *Bank Systems & Technology*, 34 (8), 30–4.

OTR Group (1997) *Do the Benefits of Datawarehousing Justify the Costs?*, Report published by OTR Group, London.

Papows, J.P. (1999) 'The payoff from knowledge management', *USBanker*, 109 (9), 80.

Parsons, A.J., Zeisser, M. and Waitman, R. (1996) 'Organising for digital marketing', *McKinsey Quarterly*, no. 4.

Partridge, M. and Perren, L. (1998) 'An integrated framework for activity-based decision making', *Management Decision*, 36 (9–10), 580–8.

Pearce, M. (1997) 'The true science of nurturing', *Marketing*, 31 July.

Peppers, D. and Rogers, M. (1995) 'A new marketing paradigm', *Planning Review*, 23 (2), 14–18.

Peppers, D. and Rogers, M. (1998) 'Customer value', *CIO*, 11 (23), 82–3.

Peppers, D., Rogers, M. and Dorf, B. (1999) 'Is your company ready for one-to-one marketing?', *Harvard Business Review*, 77 (1), 151.

Perrien, J., Filiatrault, P. and Ricard, L. (1993) 'The implementation of relationship marketing in commercial banking', *Industrial Marketing Management*, 22 (2), 141–8.

Pitt, L.F., Watson, R.T. and Kavan, C.B. (1995) 'Service quality: a measure of information systems effectiveness', *MIS Quarterly*, 19 (2), 173–87.

Pitta, D.A. (1998) 'Marketing one-to-one and its dependence on knowledge discovery in databases', *Journal of Consumer Marketing*, 15 (5), 468–80.

Power, A. and Douglas, J. (1997) 'Manufacturing the future', *Best's Review – Life-Health Insurance Edition*, 98 (4), 44–6.

PR Newswire (1998) 'Thinking machines and Paragren technologies establish strategic partnership to integrate data mining with relationship marketing software', July.

Price, C. (1999) 'Vital link in the chain of supply', *Financial Times*, 10 February, Q1: 117.

Ratcliff, P. (1998) 'Is that a bank in your pocket', *Banker*, 148 (873), 86–7.

Ravichandran, R. and Banerjee, H. (1994) 'Support for information systems usage in banks', *International Journal of Information Management*, 14 (1), 5–12.

Reed, D. (1997) 'Held to account', *Marketing Business*, 45–50.

Reed, D. (1999) 'Great expectations', *Marketing Week*, 22 (13), 57–8.

Reeves, B. (1998) 'Make new friends but keep the gold ...', *Wireless Review*, 15 (8), 28–32.

Reichheld, F.F. (1996) *The Loyalty Effect*, Boston: Harvard Business School Press.

Roscoe, D. (1999) 'The need for knowledge in customer relations', *International Journal of Customer Relationship Management*, 2(1).

Rosen, M. (1998) 'Balancing the risks and rewards of business intelligence', *ENT*, 66 (1).

Rosenthal, L. and McEachern, C. (1997) 'Getting the holistic picture', *Bank Marketing*, 29 (9), 15–21.

Rountree, D. (1997) 'Why your firm needs a data warehouse', *Insurance & Technology*, 22 (2), 36–9.

Saaksjarvi, M.V.T. and Talvinen, J.M. (1993) 'Integration and effectiveness of marketing information systems', *European Journal of Marketing*, 27 (1), 64–79.

Saarenvirta, G. (1998) 'Data mining to improve profitability', *CMA Magazine*, 72 (2), 8–12.

Saunders, J. (1999) 'Manufacturers build on CRM', *Computing Canada*, 25 (32), 17–18.

Schmittlein, D. (1995) 'Customers as strategic assets', *Financial Times*, 15 December.

Schorsch, L.L. (1994) 'You can market steel', *The McKinsey Quarterly*, 1, 111–20.

Schultz, D.E. (1993) 'Marketing from the outside in', *Journal of Business Strategy*, 14 (4), 25–9.

Schultz, D.E. (1996) 'The inevitability of integrated communications', *Journal of Business Research*, 37 (3), 139–46.

Shani, D. and Chalasani, S. (1993) 'Exploiting niches using relationship marketing', *Journal of Business & Industrial Marketing*, 8 (4), 58–66.

Sharman, P. (1996) 'ABC and the bottom line on customers', *CMA Magazine*, 70 (7), 20–4.

Shaw, R. and Stone, M. (1988) 'Competitive superiority through database marketing', *Long Range Planning*, 21 (5), 24–40.

Sheth, J.N. and Sisodia, A. (1995) 'Feeling the heat', *Marketing Management*, 4 (3), 19–33.

Simmons, L.C. (1996) 'Redefining customer service', *Mortgage Banking*, 57 (1), 163–4.

Sisodia, R.S. (1992) 'Expert marketing with expert systems', *Marketing Management*, 1 (2), 32.

Sistrum report (1998) *ROI of Investments in Sales and Marketing Systems*, Report, Hewson Consulting Group, April.

Sistrum Group (1999a) *The Sistrum Global Customer Relationship Management Project Group, Inaugural Meeting*, Hewson Consulting Group, 9 November.

Sistrum report (1999b) *Setting the Approach and Scope of Customer Relationship Management Projects*, Report, Hewson Consulting Group, November.

Softworld (1998) Sales and Marketing Annual Market Survey, Interactive Information Services, Kingston-upon-Thames, Surrey.

Spitler, R. (1997) 'Relationship management: the new paradigm', *The Journal of Lending & Credit Risk Management*, 79 (11), 51–6.

Stedman, C. (1997) 'Warehouses grow more ambitious', *Computerworld*, 31 (37), 1–2.

Stein, T. (1997) 'Closer to customers', *InformationWeek*, 630, 65–8.

Stein, T. and Caldwell, B. (1998) 'Beyond ERP – new IT agenda – a second wave of ERP activity promises to increase efficiency and transform ways of doing business, *InformationWeek*, 30 (1).

Stern, S. and Barton, D. (1997) 'Putting "custom" in customer with database marketing', *Strategy & Leadership*, 25 (3), 46–9.

Stevens, T. (1996) 'Mind your customer's business', *Industry Week*, 245 (3), 63–7.

Stone, M. and Cerasale, M. (1999) 'Automotive customer relationship management', *International Journal of Customer Relationship Management*, 2 (2).

Stone, M., Woodcock, N. and Wilson, M. (1996) 'Managing the change from marketing planning to customer relationship management', *Long Range Planning*, 29 (5), 675–83.

Stone, M., McFarlane, P., Visram, F. and Kimmel, C. (1993) 'Servicing the customer – is info tech a bridge or a barrier?', Working Paper. London: City University.

Storbacka, K. (1997) 'Segmentation based on customer profitability – retrospective analysis of retail bank customer bases', *Journal of Marketing Management*, 13 (5), 479–91.

Sweat, J. and Hibbard, J. (1999) 'Customer disservice', *Informationweek*, 739, 65–78.

Sweat, J. and Riggs, B. (1999) 'Outsiders take a shot at CRM', *Informationweek*, 750, 22.

Talmor, S. (1996) 'Mine for data', *The Banker*, 146 (842), 93.

Tapscott, D., Lowy, A. and Ticoll, D. (1998), *Blueprint to the Digital Economy*. New York: McGraw-Hill.

Tavinen, J.M., (1995) 'Information systems in marketing: identifying opportunities for new applications', *European Journal of Marketing*, 29 (1), 8–26.

techguide.com (1998) 'Achieving business success through customer relationship management'.

Thiadens, T., Saat, P., Stijger, K., Rooode, R., Klok, J., Schut, K. and Pauli, E. (1995) 'Handling a 20,000 calls-a-day telephone environment: the case of a service organization', *International Journal of Information Management*, 15 (5).

Tully, S. (1999) 'Will the Web eat Wall Street?', *Fortune*, 2 August, 112–18.

Vandenbosch, B. and Huff, S.L. (1997) 'Searching and scanning: how executives obtain information from executive information systems', *MIS Quarterly*, 21 (1), 81–107.

Vernon, M. (1998) 'Key role for IT in the marketing mix', *Financial Times*, 2 September.

Vijayan, J. (1998) 'IBM spins off customer relationship products', *Computerworld*, 32 (33), 16 August.

VP Great Western Bank (1997) quoted in Orenstein, A.F. (1997) 'Putting information to work', *Bank Systems and Technology*, 34 (8), 30–4.

Wagle, D. (1998) 'The case for ERP system', *The McKinsey Quarterly*, 98 (2).

Wang, R.Y., Lee, Y.W., Pipino, L.L. and Strong, D.M. (1998) 'Manage your information as a product', *Sloan Management Review*, 39 (4), 95–105.

Wayland, R.E. and Cole, P.M. (1994) 'Turn customer service into customer profitability; to maximise your firm's value, think of customers as a business asset', *Management Review*, 83 (7), 22–4.

Webster Jnr, F.E. (1992) 'The changing role of marketing in the corporation', *Journal of Marketing*, 56 (4).

Weisman, J.R. (1995) 'When mining customer data, don't scare off the customers', *American Banker*, 160 (51), 13.

Whiting, R. and Caldwell, B. (1999) 'Data capture grows wider', *Informationweek*, 738, 59–72.

Woods, T. and Remondi, J. (1996) 'Relationships vital for high-tech marketers', *Marketing News*, 20 May.